The West Bank

About the Book and Author

After presenting an overview of twentieth-century West Bank history, Professor Peretz provides an in-depth critical analysis of the area's development since the 1967 Israeli occupation. He compares the differing approaches to Jewish settlement of the West Bank under the Labor (1967–1977) and Likud (1977–1984) governments and identifies Israeli and Zionist infusions of economic aid to settlers under both administrations as a means of encouraging settlement and strengthening Israeli control. He also examines changes in policy since the establishment of the National Unity government. Israel's integration of West Bank transportation networks, electricity grids, and water supplies with its own is described as Dr. Peretz goes on to analyze the negative impact of government policies on the indigenous Arab population as well as on Israeli politics. Discussing the rising Palestinian national consciousness, triggered by West Bank Arab responses to Jewish settlements, he notes that young Arabs are emigrating from the West Bank in large numbers. The study concludes with an examination of viable options for the West Bank's future political status and implications for U.S. policies toward the Middle East.

Don Peretz is professor of political science at the State University of New York, Binghamton. His publications include *The Government and Politics of Israel,* Second Edition (Westview, 1984).

The West Bank
History, Politics, Society, and Economy

Don Peretz

Westview Press / Boulder and London

Westview Special Studies on the Middle East

This Westview softcover edition was manufactured on our own premises using equipment and methods that allow us to keep even specialized books in stock. It is printed on acid-free paper and bound in softcovers that carry the highest rating of the National Association of State Textbook Administrators, in consultation with the Association of American Publishers and the Book Manufacturers' Institute.

Copyright © 1986 by Westview Press, Inc.

Published in 1986 in the United States of America by Westview Press, Inc.; Frederick A. Praeger, Publisher; 5500 Central Avenue, Boulder, Colorado 80301

Library of Congress Catalog Card Number: 85-51212
ISBN: 0-8133-0297-8

Composition for this book was provided by the author.
This book was produced without formal editing by the publisher.

Printed and bound in the United States of America

 The paper used in this publication meets the minimum requirements of the American National Standard for Permanence of Paper for Printed Library Materials Z39.48-1984.

6   5   4   3   2   1

I would like to acknowledge contributions by
Bassem Abed, demography;
Vivian Bull, economy;
Emile Nakleh, West Bank Palestinians;
Ian Lustick, Israeli policies and Jewish settlement;
and Ann Lesch, consultant.

Contents

Preface

This study of the West Bank was originally undertaken for the Middle East Institute in Washington, D.C., under the terms of its contract with the U.S. Defense Intelligence Agency. The study was compiled from a series of draft working papers prepared by the author and the other contributors acknowledged below. The working papers were edited, revised, or rewritten by the author. The author holds full responsibility for the final product and for any opinions and conclusions it contains, as not all material received from the contributors was used and many of their observations were edited. Steven Heydemann copyedited and commented on first drafts; Philip Stoddard also made suggestions. The other contributors were: Bassem Abed, Vivian Bull, Ian Lustick, and Emile Nakleh; Ann Lesch was a consultant. None of these persons is responsible for the opinions or conclusions in this final product, nor should it be interpreted as necessarily representing the policy of the Defense Intelligence Agency, the Department of Defense, the U.S. government, or the views of the Middle East Institute.

Don Peretz

The West Bank

Part 1
The West Bank:
The Late Ottoman Period
Through 1967

Since the end of the 1967 Arab-Israeli war the importance of the West Bank in the politics of the Middle East has far exceeded its past historical significance or its small area and population. For many in the Middle East, both in the Arab states and in Israel, the West Bank has become the focal point of Arab-Israeli relations, the symbol of intransigence by "the other side," the proof of big power impotence and the ineffectiveness of the United Nations. Disagreements over the present and future status of the West Bank have created deep political cleavages within Israel and among Jewish communities throughout the world, among the various "moderate" and "radical" Arab states, and in the Palestine Arab nationalist movement. Indeed, internal disagreements about the status of the West Bank have produced far-reaching ideological divergencies and generated intense debate within both the Jewish and Arab nationalist movements.

Events within and policies toward the West Bank also influence larger and seemingly more important developments in the region; they affect the policies of major actors in the international arena such as the United States, the Soviet Union and the nations of Western Europe. Most recently, many analysts perceive a direct link between Israel's 1982 invasion of Lebanon, which had far-reaching consequences for the Middle East, and its policies in the West Bank. In addition, American policy has acknowledged the centrality of the West Bank, as demonstrated by the Reagan Plan of 1982 and the earlier U.S. role in such initiatives as the Camp David agreements, and U.N. Security Council resolutions 242 and 338. Thus events and policies in the West Bank strongly influence the attainment of peace between Israel and its neighbors, the future political orientation of several Arab states, the credibility of American policy in the region, and the ability of the United States to exercise international political power.

3

Since the beginning of the nineteenth century certain issues have been salient in the development of Palestine, especially as they have affected the West Bank. They include:

- The emergence of Palestinian Arab nationalism as a distinctive political movement, with the West Bank as its central focus
- The clash between Palestinian nationalism and Jewish nationalism or Zionism over the future of Palestine including the West Bank
- The question of the territorial parameters of both Palestinian and Zionist nationalisms
- The international dimensions of the Palestine problem
- The struggle between Jews and Arabs for the scarce resources of the West Bank, especially its land and its water
- The changing demographic balance between Jews and Arabs in the region

The Emergence of the West Bank

To understand the significance of these questions it is useful to trace their origins to the beginning of the century when Palestine was part of the Ottoman Empire, through the eras of the British mandate and Jordanian rule, up to the acquisition of the West Bank by Israel in the 1967 war, and to examine the patterns and trends which have emerged during each period.

The term "West Bank" is relatively new in the lexicon of international politics. Palestine, as a distinctive political term, was not widely used until after establishment of the Mandate for Palestine following World War I. The West Bank as identified today, i.e., a distinctive entity between Jordan and Israel, was not used until after the 1948 Arab-Israeli war. Before World War I both Palestine and the West Bank were different concepts.

Until the League of Nations adopted the Mandate for Palestine (and Transjordan) in 1922, Palestine was "a geographical name of rather loose application," according to the *Encyclopedia Britannica* of 1911. It generally denoted the southern third of Ottoman Syria. The Jordan River was considered the line of demarcation between Western and Eastern Palestine. Under British administration the East Bank became Transjordan and the West Bank was generally designated as the rest of Palestine, or the area in which the provisions of the Balfour Declaration of 1917 were applicable. The present West Bank grew out of a number of factors: (1) the 1948 Arab-Israeli war, (2) the subsequent Israeli-Transjordan Armistice Agreement of 1949, (3) Jordan's annexation of the areas in Western Palestine in 1950, and (4) the change in name from Transjordan to the Hashemite Kingdom of Jordan. Thereafter the kingdom was divided by the Jordan River into the East Bank and West Bank.

The West Bank began to acquire a distinctive identity as a Jordanian province after Jordan's annexation. Israel's occupation of the territory in 1967 gave it increasing significance as a bone of contention in Israeli-Arab and inter-Arab relations, and in international politics. Until Jordan's annexation today's West Bank was an integral part of Arab Palestine. Thus, in the period before 1950 it is difficult to isolate a distinctive West Bank history, pattern of economic development, or demography and social structure. True, the towns and villages of the region often were distinctive from Arab regions in Galilee, from those along the Mediterranean coast and in the southern desert (Negev). But it would be almost impossible to separate the life patterns of West Bank inhabitants from Arab Jerusalem or the other regions of Arab Palestine.

1
The Ottoman Era

Although Ottoman rule ended over 65 years ago, its consequences are still being felt in the daily life of the West Bank. Several historical factors have an immediate relevance to contemporary disputes. These include: (1) Urbanization and the development of the principal towns and cities in the West Bank, (2) the evolution of many administrative practices, (3) patterns of social organization, and (4) the emergence of land laws, many of which still exist on the West Bank today.

In late Ottoman times today's West Bank was part of the southern Syrian vilayet (province) of Beirut, and the northern sector of the Independent Sanjak (district) of Jerusalem. Beirut Vilayet included the fertile Sanjaks of Acre (not part of the West Bank) and Nablus in the north (called Balqa until 1888). The central and southern parts of Palestine had been detached from the Vilayet of Sham or Damascus and formed into the autonomous Sanjak of Jerusalem, under the control of Constantinople, as a result of European pressures, and Jerusalem's special status in international affairs.

The Ottoman Sanjaks were further subdivided into subdistricts or kazas; those including the West Bank were Nablus, Jenin, and Tulkarm in the Balqa Sanjak, and Jerusalem and Hebron as parts of the independent Jerusalem Sanjak. The Sanjak of Nablus also included part of Transjordan.

Nearly all populated parts of the West Bank were hill country which rose from the Jordan Valley whose single town of consequence was Jericho. Only a small triangle from Jenin northwards was plain country with agricultural land of more than marginal value. Before World War I, there were no Jewish agricultural settlements in the West Bank. The population was nearly all Arab with the exception of a few hundred Jews living in Hebron and a few dozen Samaritans near Nablus. According to the Ottoman census of 1914, the total population of Palestine was 689,272, of whom 60,000 were Jews; less than one percent of the West Bank was Jewish. Of the total population, 153,749 lived in the greater Nablus region and 398,362 in the Jerusalem province which included the city and areas to the south. The Christian population was concentrated in Jerusalem, Bethlehem and Ramallah and north of the West Bank in Galilee. Most of the Jewish and Christian population was urban, the Muslims, largely rural. However, by the turn of the century, the percentage of urban Muslims began to increase. Towns and cities expanded due to increased trade and commerce, and migration from over-populated rural areas.[1]

Conditions in the Ottoman provinces, including Palestine, had badly deteriorated in the early 19th century. In the West Bank the Arab population tended to cluster in the mountains and hill country as a refuge from depredations by beduins in the plains. Village feuds and the pressures of Turkish tax farmers also undermined security. The central government provided little if any protection and showed no interest in economic development in any part of Palestine. Villages found security in mutual aid and communal action. For example, land was often registered in the name of communities, the basic administrative units, rather than by individuals. Village shaykhs, who usually inherited their positions were allied with the Ottoman authorities to gain control of tax collection, giving them extensive power in rural regions.

By the end of the 19th century the Ottoman authorities began to shift their alliances from the village shaykhs to the increasingly powerful cities. Tax collection was farmed out to the highest bidders, who were usually urban notables. Consequently, by 1900 political and judicial power was shifting from the shaykhs to this new class of Ottoman allies. The village shaykh was now replaced by the new position of mukhtar, appointed by the government, and hence more dependent on and subservient to Constantinople. As the town notables developed into a distinctive social class with power extending to village networks, the villages became increasingly dependent on them.

By 1900 the Ottoman government also renewed attempts to centralize authority through the adoption of Western administrative measures. Its goals were to enhance order and stability, increase local economic production and growth without government investment, and at the same time, increase the collection of revenues. Changes in administration, tax collection and land tenure regulations did produce some economic progress.

The 1908 Ottoman constitution provided for elected city councils and for election of village mukhtars who were to be assisted by a council of elders. Male owners of immovable property were qualified to vote. But despite reforms, many of the local officials continued to be manipulated by the Ottoman governors and district officials.

Land Issues and the Changing Social Structure

A crucial issue was legislation pertaining to land, the source of most wealth and hence political power during the Ottoman era. In theory, all land belonged to the sultan or the state, acting as trustee for God; it was subdivided and classified according to various forms of usage, based on factors such as tradition and custom, quality or category of land, whether it was used individually or communally, or held in trusteeship for religious institutions. Before the later 19th century, much land was classified haphazardly, with only vague designations of ownership or entitlement to use. As part of the effort to reform and rationalize the administrative and economic systems (the Tanzimat), new legislation was introduced by Constantinople at various periods in the latter part of the century. This included the new land or *Tapu* law, giving Palestinian peasants the option of a permanent division of village-held *(Musha'a)* land that had previously been redistributed every few years. Under the new legislation, all land had to be officially registered for the first time.

What is so interesting about this law is what it reveals about the changing relationship between peasants and government and the ability of new elites to establish themselves between the two. Peasants traditionally had received very little in services from the government and nevertheless had been made to pay a significant share of their incomes as a tithe to the tax-farmers appointed by the Ottoman authorities. Even the minimal service of defense came only intermittently. . . . When the peasants heard of the new Tapu Law, they had two reactions. The first was fear—fear that it was a means to erase their anonymity within the village. They saw the law as an attempt by the government to extract higher taxes from individual households and to draft them into the imperial Army.

Their second reaction was that it was possible to maneuver around the law given the limited administrative capabilities of the central institutions. In some cases, they continued to work the land jointly but registered it under one or several names such as that of a village elder or head of a clan *(hamula)*. Frequently, peasants sought the protection of a powerful figure and sold their land or handed it free to a tax-farmer, some other strongman, or a religious foundation *(waqf)* in return for the right to continue working it. In other cases, they simply neglected to register the lands they were working.[2]

Often the results of the new situation were disastrous for the peasants, but led to the enrichment of urban notables. Lands which the villages neglected to register officially were taken over by the government and auctioned to the notables at low prices. In some cases where the lands were registered in the name of a single village elder, he might later claim ownership, thus converting the former peasant owners into tenant farmers.

Even after the late 19th and early 20th century reforms the land classification system under the Ottomans was rather chaotic. Many land transactions were never recorded in the Ottoman government's land registry and ownership was based on presumed title or informal agreements that were not officially documented. Confusion of this type led some villages to register land in the name of an urban notable, who in turn passed the land on to his heirs as though it were his property. Only after the Land Settlement of 1928, when judges in the mandatory Land Courts were given authority to rectify the confusion, was a beginning made in clarifying land ownership.

These historical developments have deep contemporary significance. The peculiarities of the land law and structure of the landholding system devised in the Ottoman era had a continuing influence on tenure and are often the cause of present disputes between the government of Israel and West Bank landholders. Former Ottoman Law, and the system resulting from it, have been manipulated to the advantage of the present occupying authorities.

As power shifted from the village shaykhs to the urban elites, local councils established under the reforms of 1908 became increasingly dominated by the urban notables who gained control of village offices and land. A number of large land-owning families, some with as much as 15,000 acres, emerged as the most visible elite. According to an Ottoman land registry prepared after 1910, in the Jerusalem and Hebron kazas twenty-six owners held 240,000 dunams (1 dunam equals about a quarter of an acre); in Nablus and Tulkarm, five owners held 121,000 dunams; in Jenin six owners held 114,000 dunams. However, a large landed estate did not necessarily coincide with a large farm. Most of the large estates were owned by absentees and the land was cultivated by tenants who rented small farms on various terms. As a result of increased concentration of landholdings in large and medium estates during the latter 19th century, the great majority of peasant farmers in the Sanjaks of Jerusalem and Nablus held less than 50 dunams per family, according to official data of 1909.[3]

Although the Ottoman government invested little of its own resources in Palestine, by the end of the 19th century it began to encourage private local investment. Export-oriented crops were increased, especially citrus and bananas, usually owned by the urban, upper middle class and notables. The authorities also attempted to establish law and order as a basis for stability and economic growth. They intervened more frequently against beduin raids, in village wars, and in control of local private militias. Increased security led to the return of villagers to plains and valleys that had been depopulated early in the 18th and 19th centuries. *Khirbes* that had been merely village outposts, increased in size and importance. As the population grew, land shortages developed, especially in the West Bank hill country. Increased population and concentration of land in larger holdings resulted in more tenant farmers, who produced about a third of all agriculture by the end of the Ottoman era. These conditions undermined traditional village self-sufficiency and started a shift of population from rural to urban centers. In the West Bank this was reflected in the growth of Nablus between 1875 and 1895 from 15,000 to 21,000.

Palestinian Arab Nationalism Under the Ottomans

Political influence in the Arab community often corresponded with ownership of large estates. Some influential families had lived in Palestine for centuries, others for only a few generations. Many were townsmen who had recently acquired wealth from business or land transactions. In the West Bank area the Abd el-Hadi family, with one branch in Nablus and another in Jenin was among the largest old families, with some 60,000 dunams, much of it beyond the West Bank. Other large land owners in the West Bank included the Zalach with large tracts in the Tulkarm district, and the Hanun and Samara families from Tulkarm.[4] Often they would acquire the properties of whole villages as a result of the new conditions. Enrichment through the acquisition of land was the main route to political power, and hence to attainment of notable status. It was these land-rich notables who became leaders of the nascent Arab nationalist movement which was beginning to take form by 1900.

Even before the Zionist movement was formally established in Europe at its first congress in 1897, notables from the West Bank were among those who petitioned the Ottoman authorities to end Jewish immigration and land purchases in Palestine. Although land in the West Bank hill country was not a primary target of Jewish acquisition and settlement, Arab notables there expressed equal concern about the growing Zionist presence as those more directly affected in areas of primary Jewish interest along the coast, in the plains, and in Galilee.

The district capital of Nablus had the most active leadership in the West Bank. Although Nablus was smaller than Jerusalem and Jaffa, less centrally located, and under Jerusalem's administrative shadow, Nablusis played an important role in administering the country during the last decades of Ottoman rule. Many Nablus notables were educated in Constantinople or abroad and several held senior positions in the Ottoman capital. Sultan Abd al-Hamid was said to have a special affection for Nablus and encouraged its local industries, especially the soap factories, and granted favors to its notables. The town's prosperity increased the size of its middle class, whose interest in education expanded. The Sultan invited several of the leading families to send their children to Constantinople for study at his expense in preparation for appointments to significant government posts.

Despite the paternal relationship between Nablus and Constantinople, several important Nablusis were active in the Arab nationalist movement, which exhibited anti-Ottoman as well as anti-Zionist tendencies. Outside Jerusalem, Nablus was the main center of national and cultural development in the region. Its two leading families, the Abd al-Hadi and Tuqan, had for years alternated the governorship of Jabal Nablus between them. When the Ottoman Decentralization Party was established in Cairo early in the century, to strive for greater local autonomy, its members included individuals from Nablus, Jenin and Tulkarm, although the overall number of Palestinians active in the nationalist movement was quite small. Most Palestinian support for the Arab congress held in Paris during 1913 (to request greater respect for Arab rights in the Ottoman Empire) also came from the Nablus district. Nationalist writers in Beirut commented on the fact that support for Arab nationalism came largely from Nablus and they attacked the Jerusalemites for their reluctance to resist Ottoman rule. The latter were probably more loyal to the Ottoman regime because of the many Jerusalem notables who had attained important roles in local administration.

During World War I all of Palestine, including the West Bank, suffered from political and natural disasters. The country was devastated by epidemics and a locust plague, the Ottoman authorities extracted heavy levies in addition to the normal tax burden, and the governor, Jemal Pasha, imposed a harsh and repressive political rule. By the end of the war, the population in the provinces which included the West Bank had declined. When the British conquered southern Palestine and Jerusalem in 1917, many local inhabitants were happy for the change.

Notes

1. Bassam Abed, "Demographic Profile of Palestine 1900–1983," unpublished manuscript August 1983.
2. Joel S. Migdal, *Palestinian Society and Politics,* Princeton, 1980, p. 13.
3. A. Granott, *The Land System in Palestine,* London, 1952, pp. 38–39.
4. Ibid.

2
The Mandatory Era

British Administration

After the British occupation of Jerusalem and establishment of Occupied Enemy Territory Administration (South)—OETA (S), the city became the center of political life and administration for Palestine. Cut off from Constantinople, Jerusalem's central position and concentration of political and administrative activity gave Palestine new meaning and identity. Even before Palestine acquired a distinct legal personality through the League of Nations Mandate, the British military administration separated the country from other areas it took from the Ottomans.

The British continued many of the administrative practices and traditions of the Ottomans, and kept in force much of the Ottoman legal system, especially land laws. When the civil administration was organized, Palestine was divided into the Northern, Southern, and Jerusalem districts. Today's West Bank included most of the Jerusalem District (except the city of Jerusalem) with subdistricts of Hebron, Bethlehem, Jerusalem, Ramallah, and Jericho, and about a third of the Northern District including subdistricts or parts of the subdistricts of Nablus, Jenin, and Tulkarm. Until 1920 each district was under a military governor with departments of finance, justice, health, agriculture, education and public works. Senior positions in the administration were filled by British officials replacing the Turks. The British opened the middle and lower ranks of the administration to native Palestinians, both Jews and Arabs.

Even after a civil administration took over on July 1, 1920, many former military government officers remained in their posts. Practices of the military administration continued until after ratification of the Mandate for Palestine by the League of Nations in 1922 and its coming into force in September 1923.

Under the Mandate, Palestine was governed by a quasi-constitution in the form of an Order-in-Council, a form of legislation used in other foreign countries under British control that did not require approval by

13

the British parliament. This type of government was identical to that of the Crown Colony. It gave Palestine's High Commissioner the authority and prerogatives of a Royal Governor. He was commander-in-chief of the armed forces, and had broad executive, legislative, and administrative powers, limited only by the terms of the Mandate, the Order-in-Council, and by occasional instructions from the Colonial Office in London. Although the High Commissioner was assisted by an Executive Council, he was not in any way bound by its recommendations. His powers included trusteeship over state property, the right to grant pardons to criminals and to deport political offenders.

Under the Mandate a new system of courts was organized including magistrate, district and land courts and a Supreme Court. Judges in the magistrate courts were Palestinian. Other judges were British.

District Commissioners and the department heads in the central administration at Jerusalem were British, several from the Military Government. The police force, headed by British officers, was mostly Arab, although after the 1921 uprising, several hundred British constables were enlisted.

In the lower civil service ranks the mandatory government gradually replaced British officials with Palestinians. Christian Arabs were the best represented and Muslims the least, except in the railroads where they provided many unskilled laborers. By 1924, Christian Arabs, who were 10 percent of the population held over 30 percent of government positions; Jews, who were 15 percent, occupied 20 percent, and the Muslim 75 percent of the population held less than 15 percent of government positions.

The Mandate provided for local government and during the 1920s District Commissioners recommended that many villages set up their own councils. The first High Commissioner, Sir Herbert Samuel, observed that many Arab villages were interested in self-government as a way to promote and develop their own schools.

The Ottoman millet system, which promoted extensive local autonomy along religious-national lines, was adapted by the mandatory government to the new conditions in Palestine. During the Ottoman era, the Muslim community had been under the ultimate jurisdiction of the Islamic authorities in Constantinople where the government reigned supreme in all matters relating to Muslims. With the separation of Palestine from the Ottoman Empire, it was necessary to establish an authoritative body to direct Muslim affairs. Thus, in 1921, a Supreme Muslim Council was set up with complete control over Waqfs and the Sharia establishment (Muslim religious courts). As a result the Muslim hierarchy in Palestine gained far more control over their religious affairs than they held during Ottoman times.

The British political style in Palestine resembled that in other colonies. The authorities attempted to forge political alliances with the local population through notable families and to establish a working relationship with them to maintain stability. Thus, the notables who had attained status and power under the Ottomans remained influential during the Mandate. The Husayni family was rewarded with control of Muslim religious affairs by appointment as head of the Central Waqf Committee and with the presidency of the Sharia Appeals Court in Jerusalem. The title of Grand Mufti was devised and bestowed on Haj Amin al-Husayni, head of the Muslim religious system, a title that added prestige, especially since the Mufti's headquarters was in Jerusalem, which had acquired a central role among Palestinian Muslims.

The Mufti was later able to consolidate his power throughout the Palestine Arab community. Family or hamula connections linked leaders of the smaller villages with the larger ones, and they in turn were woven into the family networks of the larger towns. When Haj Amin al-Husayni became Grand Mufti and President of the Supreme Muslim Council, he used the extensive funds of the Waqf (estimated at 12.75 percent of the country's total resources) to strengthen these links. In the West Bank area Nablus was a principal beneficiary of the Mufti's largesse because of his close ties there whereas Hebron, where his following was weak, was neglected.

In terms of the general conditions of the area, British policies had a stabilizing effect. Beduin raids from across the Jordan River were ended. The road network was greatly extended, largely for security purposes, legislation was introduced in order to decrease dependency of the fellah on large land owners. Public health measures contributed greatly to extending life expectancy resulting in Arab population growth. Between 1931 and 1946 the infant mortality rate among Muslims decreased from 187 to 128 per 1,000. By 1947 the Arab population had increased over 120 percent, one of the highest rates of increase in the world.

Palestine Demography

The British conducted the first modern census of Palestine in December 1922. It showed a total population of 757,182; 78 percent Muslim, 9.6 percent Christian, 11 percent Jewish and 1 percent other. The Muslim population was distributed in urban and rural areas throughout the country; Christians were concentrated in northern Palestine (Galilee) and in West Bank cities of Jerusalem, Ramallah, Bethlehem and their environs; Jews were largely urban, mostly in Jerusalem, Tel-Aviv, Jaffa, in the Jerusalem-Jaffa corridor, along the coast, and in the north.

The West Bank was not an attractive site for Jewish settlement in this period. The Jews constituted less than one percent of the West Bank. There was no Jewish population in Ramallah, Nablus and Jenin, only 0.2 percent in Hebron, 0.1 percent in Bethlehem and 0.14 percent in Tulkarm. Whereas the Jewish population increased from about 10 to more than 30 percent of Palestine's population during the Mandate, it remained at about one percent in the West Bank, not including Jerusalem, throughout this period.[1]

As the Arab population expanded, pressure on the land grew resulting in migration from rural areas to the cities and increasing pressure by large land owners on their tenants. Jewish land purchases also helped to inflate prices and to increase demands for land. Pressure was less in the West Bank—where there were many fewer Jewish settlements— than along the coast, in the plains and in Galilee. The greatest rates of population increase and in urban growth were outside the West Bank. Throughout the mandatory era there was a shift of population from east to west with the result that West Bank cities including Bethlehem, Nablus, Hebron and Jenin and their dependent villages grew less rapidly than coastal cities like Haifa and Jaffa. The center of population gravity moved from Jerusalem, in the center, outward. In 1922 Jerusalem had the largest Arab population, but by 1944 it had declined to the third largest Arab city, outranked by Haifa and Jaffa.

Arab Economy

Agriculture

Agriculture remained the principal Arab occupation. There was moderate development of industry, mainly handicrafts, but only a few large scale enterprises. A major source of employment was the mandatory government, which by 1939 hired some 15,000 daily workers, not including government clerks. During World War II this number increased more than five times, at the same rate as burgeoning military expenditures.

Most of the populated area in the West Bank was in the hill country. The two principal West Bank towns, Hebron and Nablus, are located in hill regions, the former in the Judean hills, the latter in Samaria. The Judean hill area was the least fertile with primarily subsistence agriculture. Because farming there required extensive clearance of stone and terracing, little wheat was grown, and herds of sheep and goats were permitted to use the sparse pastures. The chief crops of most Judean villages were olives, grapes, figs, apricots and vegetables (grown to supply the market towns of Jerusalem, Hebron and Bethlehem).

Hebron was only fifteen miles north of the line demarcating the limit of non-nomadic settlement.

Although Samaria was more productive than Judea, it too survived at close to subsistence levels. A fertile pocket extended northwest from Nablus and in the environs of the town there was enough rain to cultivate wheat and barley. The other main crops were olives, figs and apricots.

During the Mandate there was no systematic survey of cultivable land; the last estimates during the 1940s were based on a tax survey of 1932-34. A survey undertaken by the Jewish National Fund (no date—probably 1940-41) estimated that more than half the hill country was cultivable. According to Robert Nathan "shockingly little [was] known in Palestine about the magnitude of Arab farm employment."[2] Estimates of Arab employment in agriculture ranged from 61 to 80 percent. Up to 1940 the absolute numbers of Arabs in agriculture increased yearly, although evidence suggested that the percentage employed in farming began to decline during the 1930s, probably due to the rapid increase of population and its movement from rural to urban areas.

By the end of the mandate there were an estimated 80,000 Arab farms in Palestine, most of them between 50 and 100 dunams, working at subsistence levels. In 1930 the Johnson-Crosbie report estimated that the average annual income from such a typical farm was 35 Palestine pounds a year for a family that owned its land and 20 Palestine pounds for a tenant family. About 30 percent of this income was used for rent, and average indebtedness was equal to annual per capita income.

Although the fellah was impoverished, the overall position of agriculture during the Mandate improved. Arab-cultivated area increased from five million to more than seven million dunams. The emphasis shifted from sheep and goats to cattle, production of olives, fruit, vegetables and poultry greatly expanded, and production for urban markets developed on an extensive scale.

During World War II there was a price revolution in Palestinian agriculture. The government devised a food policy based on restricting imports, with emphasis on local production. The greatest price increases were in Arab products, especially cereals, olive oil, eggs and mutton. Overall the increase was more than fivefold between 1938 and 1944. The increase in prices for agricultural products facilitated payment of a large part of the debts accumulated by the fellah, often over generations, and led to an overall increase in living standards.

Under the British Mandate a major effort was made to clarify issues of land tenure and classification. During the Ottoman era, land disputes were frequent. In 1928, the British enacted a "Land Settlement Ordinance" which gave judges of Land Courts, established during the Mandate, authority to make clear-cut decisions on ownership and thus to end much of the ambiguity underlying land disputes. Rules were laid down for determining rights of ownership or possession and for issue of title deeds, based on a new land survey. Although ownership of only a small part of total agricultural land was "settled" by the end of the Mandate, some of the confusion and ambiguity was cleared up in certain areas where "land settlement" was carried out under the 1928 ordinance. In other areas, such as the southern half of the future West Bank, much confusion over land ownership would continue throughout the Jordanian period.

Industry

There was limited expansion of the small industrial sector in the Arab economy during the Mandate. Most production was for local use in handicraft shops without power-driven machinery. The few exceptions were the manufacture of irrigation pumps, milling machinery and building materials. The only significant manufactured export was olive oil soap which acquired a market in surrounding countries because it was free of animal fat and thus met Muslim ritual requirements. Nablus was the chief center of the soap industry. The single modern industry was flour milling, although with British guidance the use of machinery was also introduced in manufacture of cigarettes and building materials. As the population increased, the demand for building materials led to expansion of stone quarrying and production of bricks, pipes and tiles. Nonetheless, industrial labor remained a small percentage of the total work force. By 1939 only about 6,000 people were employed in the 350 Arab enterprises counted in the government census. During World War II there was a fourfold increase of Arab industry, mostly in textile and shoe manufacturing; by the end of the war the number of workers in Arab-owned industries had increased to between 10,000 and 11,000, about a fifth of the number of employees in the Jewish industrial sector. In 1942 an estimated 85,000 to 100,000 Arabs were employed in manual and some 30,000 in nonmanual work such as clerical, office and the like.[3]

During World War II with the increase in military construction, there was a fourfold increase among Arabs employed in building trades. Arabs were dominant in construction for the army because it did not require a high level of skills. According to official estimates in 1942, 63,000 persons were employed in construction representing 10.6 percent of Palestine's total labor force, double the percentage employed in building during 1936. This was a fourfold increase of Arab construction workers.

Housing construction in the Arab sector failed to keep up with the rate of population increase. In the West Bank, where the increase was not as great as in other Arab sectors, there was little change in housing conditions, except that they became more dense. Rural Arabs continued to live in densely built-up villages rather than in isolated farms. In the Arab towns, "schools provide[d] one of the most flagrant examples of the inadequacy of public buildings." Very few new schools were constructed. Most were in state domain buildings inherited from the Ottoman era or in rented private houses. Because of the pressure of increased population, students were turned away with "small classrooms . . . overcrowded to the extent of being a menace to public health. Of the 26,000 school places in Arab town schools in 1940, less than half were classified by [the] Government as satisfactory accommodations."[4]

Arab Trade Unions

With such a small percentage of the population employed in industry, Arab labor unions were at best fringe activities. By the end of the Mandate, when Arabs outnumbered Jews more than two to one, the number of organized Arab laborers was a seventh of those organized in the Jewish sector. Labor unions were unwelcome to the middle class Arab political leadership. Aside from the 2,500 workers organized in the Arab section of the Histadrut, there were two other independent Arab unions, the Palestine Arab Workers Association founded at Haifa in 1925 (it had some 5,000 members by 1944), and the Federation of Arab Trade Unions and Labour Societies founded in 1930 with 3,000 members by 1944.

To help overcome "the lack of responsible guidance and leadership in the Arab trade union movement," the mandatory government created a Labor Department in 1942. It organized an Arab Workers' conference in 1943, at which one of the department officials (a former British trade union officer) called for establishment of a single trade federation with a membership of 50,000. A union of Arabs employed by the armed forces and in the government tobacco control administration was also formed with government assistance, bringing the total number of organized Arab workers up to 16,500 by 1944. The Labor Department also helped to form independent unions in Nablus, Nazareth and Ramallah; Nablus was the largest with over 1,000 members. With government assistance the Palestine Arab Workers Association, which had fallen on hard times, was reorganized and new chapters were opened in Nablus and Bethlehem.[5]

Political Life

The West Bank, especially Nablus, was very active in the political life of the Arab community. Activity during the mandatory era went through three distinct phases. The first was one of limited political mobilization, when the urban and land owning elite played the most prominent roles. It lasted from 1917 until the early 1930s. The second phase, lasting until 1939, saw rapid mobilization of radical groups, led by youths, religious figures and peasants who challenged the leadership of the elite and adopted militant tactics, especially during the Arab rebellion in the late 1930s. The last phase was political disintegration during the 1940s terminating with the flight of the Palestinian refugees in 1947–48. During this third phase most political parties were banned by the British and the key leaders were exiled. Throughout this period the efficacy of Arab politics was seriously constrained by intra-communal rivalries. Personality clashes, competition between rural and urban notables and tension between younger modernists and older traditionalists all undermined the influence of the nationalist movement. These factors continue to hinder Palestinian politics today.[6]

Phase One: The Arab Executive

The first phase was dominated by the Arab Executive representing leading Christian and Muslim families, the notables who had been leaders during the latter Ottoman era. The Arab Executive, originally composed of 24 Muslims and Christians, was established as a permanent organization at Haifa in 1920 by the third Palestine Arab Congress (the first was in February 1919). The Congress was a meeting of Muslim-Christian Associations that were formed during the early days of British occupation to protest against the proposed Jewish National Home.

The Executive continued the series of Congresses, meeting in 1921, 1922, and 1923. The more militant members called for a campaign of noncooperation with the British, including a boycott of the advisory council and refusal to pay taxes. Only the boycott was implemented; land owners and merchants feared that their property would be seized if they challenged government tax regulations.

In the West Bank, Nablus was the focal point of the burgeoning Palestine national movement. It lagged behind the coastal cities and Jerusalem in modernization because patterns of traditional society were stronger there. Although the Christian minority of several hundred Greek-Orthodox was decreasing in Nablus, it was a sufficient number to join with Muslim notables in forming a Muslim-Christian Association. According to some observers, ". . . in Nablus . . . the spirit of national

Arab unity was stronger than in other parts of Palestine".[7] When the Arab Executive was set up, the leader of one of the two main rival factions in Nablus was elected as a member. Haj Tawfiq Hamad, leader of one faction stood out as the main figure in the nationalist camp, and was a member of the Executive; Haydar Bey Tuqan led the opposing faction, and was the mainstay of opposition groups in the Nablus area.

The Husaynis were the most influential family in the Arab Executive; they presided over it and several of the Congresses. They also became the acknowledged spokesmen of the Muslim-Christian Associations and headed several Palestinian Arab delegations abroad. After Haj Amin al-Husayni attained the presidency of the Muslim Supreme Council and the title of Mufti of Jerusalem, the Husaynis became the dominant force in the national movement; his supporters were known as Councilites.

By 1922 a nationalist opposition began to form around the second most powerful Jerusalem Muslim family, the Nashashibis, who were the chief Husayni rivals during the late Ottoman period. They headed an association of National Muslim Societies made up of Arab mayors, land owners, and wealthy merchants, as a counterpoise to the Muslim-Christian Associations. While initially opposing partnership with Christians in the Arab Executive, the National Muslim Association, dependent on the British administration for political influence, adopted a conciliatory attitude and even lowered the pitch of its opposition to Jewish immigration into Palestine. Hoping to undermine the Councilites and to resist Zionism from within the terms of the Mandate, the Opposition formed the National Party in 1923. During 1924 several peasant parties were created in rural areas, including the Nablus, Jenin and Hebron regions with Zionist financial assistance. These groups sought to cooperate with the government and wanted equality between urban and rural factions; they also demanded greater attention to rural problems. Within a few years these parties disintegrated when their source of Zionist support dwindled due to lack of funds and changing Zionist policies.

The Councilites and Opposition factions attempted to extend their influence by establishing village networks and alliances with local notables and family clans. The struggle was played out in elections for the municipal councils and in the battle for control of the finances of the Sharia establishment and Waqfs. Haj Amin al-Husayni had a decided advantage in this conflict. He controlled finances in the Muslim establishment. Nevertheless, the Nashashibis did gain the upper hand in many local elections, including Nablus, where members of the Tuqan and Abd al-Hadi families opposed the Councilites.

In the West Bank the Husayni-Nashashibi clash highlighted traditional urban-rural rivalries. In several towns strong Opposition groups were formed to counter the Councilites who were perceived as representing the urban elite. In the Jenin and Tulkarm regions strong rural families, including the Jarrar in the villages of the Jenin subdistrict, and Abu Hantash, were active in the Opposition. They were joined in the Hebron area by the Hudayb family.

The Opposition was further strengthened during the mid-1920s by growing internal disputes among the Councilites, especially over the tactics of Haj Amin. When Abd al-Latif Salah, the Nablus district representative in the Supreme Muslim Council, saw that he was losing local support, he broke with the Nablus Muslim-Christian Association and established his own organization. Both in Hebron and Nablus dissatisfaction with the financial management and disbursements of the Mufti increased. By the mid-1920s the tide was beginning to turn against the Councilites, as demonstrated by the increasing number of municipal council election victories of the Opposition. There were also many younger nationalists dissatisfied with the Muslim establishment. In 1931 the Nablus Muslim Christian Association changed its name to the Patriotic Arab Association, representing the desire of young militants to express a new nationalist spirit, less anchored in the traditional communal structure.

Hebron too was a center of opposition during the 1920s and early 1930s. There were several disputes between administrators of local waqfs and the Supreme Muslim Council over the use of resources. Hebron sent no representatives to the first three congresses and contributed little to the Arab Executive in the early years.

An attempt was made to reconcile the diverse Palestinian Arab factions at the Seventh Palestine Arab Congress held in Jerusalem in 1928. Both Councilites and the Opposition participated and a substantial number of young, reform-minded politicians were represented. Moderate resolutions were passed, calling for the establishment of a representative assembly with tacit acceptance of the Mandate.

1929 Riots

These efforts at conciliation were aborted by the Wailing Wall riots and violence elsewhere in the country during 1929. The Wailing Wall incident stemmed from protracted and tense disagreements between Jews and Muslims over this holy site, which included both the Muslim Haram al-Sharif and the remnants of the Jewish temple wall. The clash marked a new phase in Palestine's political history. It deepened the rift between Jews and Muslims, intensified Arab use of violence, and internationalized the Arab-Jewish conflict more than ever before. The incident symbolized the complex, deep components of the struggle—its nationalist, religious, and ethnic dimensions. One consequence was the killing by Hebron Arabs of more than sixty Jewish men, women and children, the wounding of fifty more, and desecration of their synagogue. The massacre ended several centuries of Jewish presence in the town and became a symbol of Arab treachery to militant Jewish nationalists. These events hardened the Zionist stand against political concessions to the Arabs and caused the British to halt their discussions of a legislative council. They also reflected the political unsophistication of Arab mass sentiment, since the Hebron Jews were not Zionist.

Phase Two: The Militant Trend

The second or radicalized phase of the national movement occurred during the 1930s. Boy Scout groups, Young Muslim societies, and two new political parties, the Pan-Arab Independence Party and the Youth Congress, all pressed the Arab Executive to adopt a more militant stand, and pressured it into supporting nonviolent demonstrations in Jaffa and Jerusalem during October 1933. However, with the death of its elderly chief, Musa Kazim al-Husayni in 1934 the Arab Executive's importance waned. Relations between Councilites and Opposition became strained again and several new competing nationalist groups appeared on the scene.[8]

In addition to the Independence Party and Youth Congress, there were the Reform Party and National Bloc. The latter was the personal vehicle of the moderately influential Nablus politician, Abdul Latif Salah. The councilite followers of the Mufti formed the Palestine Arab Party, principal heir to the Arab Executive, and the Nashashibi Opposition established the National Defense Party. The mayor of Jerusalem, Dr. Husayn Fakhri al-Khalidi, led the Reform Party.

Although rivalry among these factions was intense, a series of internal and international developments converged to unify the Arab nationalists by the mid-1930s. With the rise of Hitler in Germany, Jewish immigration to Palestine increased. As the numbers of Jews in the country grew, the presence of the Zionist enterprise became more visible. Jewish towns and cities expanded, Jewish agricultural and industrial enterprises multiplied, and Jewish political demands were sharpened. Land sales by Arabs to Jews were more frequent.

Not only was there an increase in land sales to Jews in this second phase, these sales also changed their character. During the 1920s most land was purchased from big land owners, many of whom were not Palestinian, but Lebanese and Syrian. Some of the land in these transactions was uninhabited although some villages were displaced. Land sold by Palestinians during the 1930s was usually more cultivated and inhabited, resulting in more frequent disputes between Jewish buyers and former Arab tenants.

Most Jewish land acquisitions were outside the West Bank for several reasons. The pattern of Arab ownership in the West Bank differed from that in parts of Galilee and the coastal plain where Zionist purchases were concentrated. Instead of large tracts concentrated in the hands of a small number of absentees whose willingness to part with their property was largely a function of the price offered, land in the West Bank hill country was more evenly distributed among individual farmers, clans and villages. The urban infrastructures supportive of modern living patterns, industry, and commerce—well developed in the coastal areas—were, by comparison, primitive in the mountainous West Bank. Moreover, West Bank agricultural areas were relatively densely populated. Nablus and Jerusalem, centers of Palestinian nationalist sentiment, were less receptive to a Jewish influx, and the Hebron area was known for its deeply rooted Muslim character. In these areas the cultural and economic resistance to parting with ancestral lands was reinforced by intense political and religious opposition to Jewish settlement and to the Zionist efforts to build the Jewish national home.

By the end of 1935 and the beginning of 1936 political tension in both Arab and Jewish communities rose sharply. After years of hesitation the British mandatory government declared its intent to establish a Palestine Legislative Council, but the Parliament in London, under pressure from the Jewish Agency, blocked the proposal as "premature" undermining the reformist approach to the nationalist problem. In neighboring Egypt and Syria, nationalists seemed to be making headway so that by 1936 they had received promises of concessions, in contrast to the frustration of nationalist hopes in Palestine.

The Arab Revolt

These rising tensions broke into violence during April 1936. After two Jews were murdered, a cycle of Jewish reprisals and assaults on Arabs, and Arab attacks on Jews was started. Now the number of Arab nationalists increased, who opposed any compromise short of total independence and who rejected negotiations with either Jews or British. By April 20, 1936, a national committee was created in Nablus calling for a general strike until the British agreed to accept the full nationalist program. A network of national committees in Arab towns and villages throughout Palestine was formed. Their demands were endorsed by the heads of five political parties, and within four days the Independence Party also joined to form a permanent ten-man executive later called the Arab Higher Committee, under the presidency of Haj Amin. It reiterated the three basic demands of the nationalists: prohibition of Jewish immigration, a ban on land transfers from Arabs to Jews, termination of the Mandate and its replacement by an independent national government responsible to a representative council.

A congress of local "national committees" met in May and approved a more radical program. It called for civil disobedience, nonpayment of taxes, and a halt to municipal government. Eventually the strike halted virtually all business and transport. Local committees organized food distribution to the towns. Although Arab government officials continued to work, they contributed ten percent of their salaries to the strike fund. Local actions became a country-wide general strike, paralyzing government operations throughout Arab Palestine. However, after six months the strike failed to coerce the British into a new policy. Furthermore, the strike galvanized the Jewish Community (Yishuv) into counteraction resulting in the replacement of Arab workers and services in many sectors of the Jewish economy. The Arab closing of Jaffa port, for example, led to the establishment of a new Jewish port in Tel Aviv.

Within a month the general strike escalated into an armed rebellion as Arab guerrilla bands were activated. Their targets were Jewish sections of the cities and settlements, and various British installations. The guerrilla forces were supplemented by Arab volunteers from abroad; the most notable was an Iraqi officer, Fawzi al-Qawuqji. He was the acknowledged commander of the various regional commands, although Arab fighting forces were never integrated under a strictly hierarchical military organization.

The West Bank was one of the three centers of nationalists who advocated armed struggle against the Yishuv and the British. In Jerusalem followers of the Mufti were organized in *al-Jihad al Muqaddas;* in Haifa and Galilee Muslim bands were led by leaders of the Haifa Young Men's Muslim Association, especially by followers of Sheikh Izz al-Din al-Qassam, who was killed shortly after he had launched a guerrilla operation from the mountains near Jenin the previous November. In the West Bank the militants were concentrated in the Tulkarm area where they were guided by young educated nationalists, many of them teachers and health officers in the civil service.

The village bands were initially successful in using guerrilla tactics, derailing trains, mining and barricading roads, severing telephone lines and the Iraq Petroleum Company pipeline to Haifa. They received active support from neighboring Arab states where Committees for the Defense of Palestine were established.

The High Commissioner responded by imposing a regime of drastic emergency legislation authorizing arrest and seizures without warrants, deportation of dissidents, imposition of curfews and censorship. The principle of collective punishment was introduced and many of the strike leaders and other prominent Arabs were interned. In response to an appeal from the Jewish Agency, the Yishuv was permitted to increase its defense forces, the number of Jewish police officers was doubled, and a new Jewish supernumerary police force was formed.[9]

Partition Plans: The Arab Response

In Great Britain the revolt led to appointment of a Palestine Royal Commission (the Peel Commission) to investigate the causes of unrest and to make recommendations for resolving of the problem. The Commission concluded in July 1937 that each community had such a distinct political identity and socioeconomic characteristics that it seemed impossible for them to live in a unitary state. Each feared domination by the other, and each sought statehood on its own land. Nevertheless, the two communities were geographically intermixed, both in rural areas and the cities. The Commission recommended partition as the only solution, but recognized that it would be difficult to draw lines that would satisfy either party and that major population displacements might ensue. In fact, the Jewish Agency insisted that the 250,000 Arabs in Galilee be removed at British expense so that the Arab population in the proposed Jewish state would not be too large. Under the proposed partition scheme none of the area that now comprises the West Bank would have been in the Jewish state.

Neither Zionist nor Arab leaders were totally satisfied with the recommendations of the Royal commission, which sparked internal disagreements in both camps. Only a few days before the release of the report, the Nashashibi-sponsored National Defense party formally dissociated itself from the Arab Higher Committee, charging the Mufti with responsibility for intimidating Arabs who disagreed with his policies. The Councilites, on the other hand, accused the Nashashibi followers of betrayal and of support for a secret plan to accept partition, with the intent of placing the Arab state under the rule of Amir Abdullah of Transjordan. The basis for this suspicion was growing friendship between the Hashemite ruler and the Nashashibis, a relationship that was to become the basis of even deeper hostilities among Palestinian Arabs.

While the Nashashibis seemed willing to accept some form of partition, the National Defense party rejected the specifics of the Peel plan as incompatible with Arab nationalist aspirations and prejudicial to Palestinian interests. Publication of the recommendations triggered the second phase of the Palestinian Arab rebellion in late 1937. It soon became clear to Great Britain that partition could not be implemented peacefully. The British responded with appointment of still another commission designated to develop specific plans for dividing the country.

The Palestine Partition Commission (the Woodhead Commission) finished its work in October 1938, concluding that the Peel plan was impractical. Rather, it proposed a new division with proposals that were even less acceptable to Arabs or Jews.

During the second phase of the Arab revolt hundreds of local politicians and members of the Arab Higher Committee were arrested. The Committee was banned and Haj Amin was removed as president of the Supreme Muslim Council. He and his cousin, Jamal al-Husayni, head of the Palestine Arab Party, escaped to Lebanon. The subsequent vacuum in the leadership of local notables soon brought the rebellion under the control of peasant guerrilla commanders. From late 1937 until the end of 1938 a major rural revolt swept across Palestine. Much of the countryside fell under guerrilla control and at times they even dominated parts of cities, including Jerusalem, Jaffa and Beersheba. By mid-1938 the British sent military reinforcements that systematically combed the towns and villages, made mass arrests, demolished houses of suspects, and fenced in the border with Syria which had been the route for military supplies to the rebels.

As leadership of the rebellion shifted from urban notables to Muslim villagers in the lower socioeconomic strata, tensions between cities and rural areas increased. The common élan and enthusiasm that had marked the early phases of the revolt deteriorated. Heavy losses incurred by the middle class, professionals and merchants during the general strike, and the escalation of guerrilla demands upon towns and villages, cooled the enthusiasm of many for the revolt. Often guerrilla treatment of the villagers turned them into informers for the British against the rebel fighters. These tensions were underscored in the words of one rebel commander who wrote to his followers: "If we do not decide to kill some of the rural notables, the Revolt will be doomed."[10] Indeed, these internecine clashes between rebels and their village hosts killed more Palestine Arabs than were killed either by Jews or the British.

As socioeconomic distinctions within the Palestine Arab community intensified the nationalist uprising acquired many aspects of a social revolution. After occupying several towns in November 1938, the guerrilla forces decreed a moratorium on debts and suspended all court actions related to debt payments. Violation of this order was punishable by fine and flogging for a first offense and by execution for a second. The moratorium was a boon to peasants with debts but a severe financial blow to urban money lenders. Another such order warned creditors or their agents to keep away from villages for debt collection and not to take any legal steps against debtors. A further measure identifying the rebels with the urban lower classes and village poor was a declaration canceling all rents. The rebels even imposed a "people's" dress code ordering the townsmen to replace the traditional Ottoman red fez *(tarbush)* with the rural beduin headcloth *(kafiyyah* and *igal)*. Most townsmen complied with the order including Christians and those in the Westernized sector. Lawyers even applied for permission to wear the village headdress in courts lest they suffer retribution. In many places Christian women wore the veil instead of European millinery to blend in with the prevailing nationalist environment. The argument presented for replacement of the fez was that it was a heritage of Ottoman repression while the kafiyya and igal were true national headgear, true symbols of Arabism. In towns controlled by the rebels they often imposed a strict regime. In some areas they forbade the inhabitants to use electricity because it was produced by an Anglo-Jewish company.[11]

One of the most significant phenomena to develop during the Arab rebellion was the rise of Sheikh Izz al-Din al-Qassam's movement, referred to above. Al-Qassam has been glorified as a founder of the "Arab Resistance," the first Arab "martyr" in the cause of Palestinian independence. Although al-Qassam was killed in a clash with the British in November 1935, he became the symbol of revolution and a legend among his followers, especially among the large numbers of displaced peasants crowded into the shantytowns and slums around Haifa and Jaffa.

Studies of leadership in nationalist institutions and in organizations of the rebellion show how prominent was the West Bank, especially Nablus. Porath's survey of 282 officers in the rebel movement shows that of 61 townsmen, Nablus led with 17, Jerusalem was second with only 12, Hebron and Jenin were fourth and sixth respectively. Porath notes that in Nablus a group of teachers from the al-Najah school were advisors to the guerrilla chiefs. Of the 183 villagers who were rebel officers, 29 were from the Tulkarm-Qalqilya region, 24 from the Jenin region, 20 from the Nablus region, and 7 from the Hebron region.[12]

Phase Three: The Decline of Arab Palestine

As World War II approached, the Arab revolt in Palestine lost its momentum and began to flicker out. The British increased their military forces in the country and intensified their anti-guerrilla campaigns. Not only were the guerrillas divided among themselves, but increasingly they were met with hostility by Arab towns and villages that had formerly offered them hospitality.

A large number of Palestinian political and military leaders were exiled by the British and could no longer carry out their leadership functions. Much of the wind was taken out of the militant nationalist sails by the British White Paper of 1939 which made significant concessions to the Arabs. Although it was denounced by the Mufti and his followers, it contained sufficient promise for many Palestine Arabs to give it tacit support. It was regarded with near unanimity by the Yishuv and the world Zionist Organization as a disaster for the Jewish National Home. The document promised independence in ten years, conditions permitting. After filling a five-year Jewish immigration quota the Arabs would have to approve further Jewish immigration. Jewish land purchases were limited to a tiny sector of Palestine, in areas already heavily populated by the Jews.

By the end of the 1930s the Arab community entered its third and final phase of political disintegration. From 1937 until 1945 all Arab political parties were banned except the Nashashibi National Defense party and most of the top leaders were either exiled or in detention. Political organization took place only indirectly, through labor unions, chambers of commerce or municipalities, all of them weak and limited vehicles. When Jamal al-Husayni, the Mufti's cousin, head of the moribund Palestine Arab Party returned from exile in 1946, he tried to resume control over the nearly defunct Arab Higher Committee, but his authority was contested by Independence Party leaders and some of the remaining independent politicians. The surrounding Arab countries had to intercede to reestablish a common Palestinian Arab front.

By the end of World War II, the political power balance in Palestine and on the international scene had turned against the Arab community. It decidedly favored the goals of the Zionist movement. Attempts to limit Jewish immigration and to implement the 1939 White Paper sparked widespread civil disobedience, then military resistance by the Yishuv, finally persuading Great Britain to turn the problem over to the newly formed United Nations. After lengthy debates and new investigation committees, the U.N. General Assembly recommended partition of Palestine in November 1947. The country was to be divided into a Jewish state consisting of the coastal plain, eastern Galilee, and most of the southern Negev. Its 32 percent of Palestine's population would receive about 55 percent of the land. The Arabs would retain central Galilee, the mountain district (most of which was later to become the West Bank), the southern coast (some of which was later called the Gaza Strip), and the city of Jaffa. Jerusalem and its environs would become an international enclave under U.N. Trusteeship.

Whereas the Yishuv and most of the Zionist organization received the partition proposal with jubilation, the Arabs rejected it outright as a violation of their self-determination. The British attempted to stay aloof, arguing that they would only endorse a plan acceptable to both sides. Within Palestine, civil war between the Yishuv and Arabs erupted. As the U.N. date fixed for the end of the Mandate, May 14, 1948, approached, fighting intensified: Each side attempted to consolidate its holdings before the British departed.

By the end of the Mandate, the Jewish forces were on the offensive, controlling some areas outside the anticipated Jewish state even before Arab armies invaded. Following the first Arab-Israeli war, they eventually controlled nearly 8,000 of Palestine's 10,000 square miles, nearly 2,000 more than allocated to the Jewish state in the partition resolution. After a series of cease-fires, and the negotiation of separate Armistice Agreements between Israel and Egypt, Lebanon, Transjordan and Syria, Palestine was divided into three parts: the new State of Israel, the Egyptian-controlled Gaza Strip, and the West Bank under Jordan. During the fighting more than 700,000 Arabs left the territory held by Israel for the surrounding Arab states where they became refugees. For all practical purposes, the Arab state envisaged in the U.N. Partition Resolution was aborted and a new entity was created—the West Bank.

Notes

1. Bassam Abed, "Demographic Profile of Palestine 1900–1983" op.cit.

2. Robert R. Nathan, Oscar Gass, Daniel Creamer, *Palestine: Problem and Promise, An Economic Study,* Washington D.C., 1946, p. 194.

3. Ibid., p. 231.

4. Ibid., pp. 246–247.

5. Ibid., p. 297.

6. Ann Mosely Lesch, *Arab Politics in Palestine, 1917–1939: The Frustration of a Nationalist Movement,* Ithaca 1979, pp. 17–20 and passim.

7. Y. Porath, *The Emergence of the Palestinian Arab Nationalist Movement 1918–1929,* London, 1974, p. 87.

8. Ann M. Lesch, op. cit., Chapter 5; Y. Porath, *The Palestinian Arab Nationalist Movement 1929–1939: From Riots to Rebellion,* London, 1977, passim.

9. Ibid., Porath, passim.

10. Ibid., Porath, p. 266.

11. Ibid., Porath, pp. 265–269.

12. Ibid., Porath, pp. 260–264, 388–403.

The Jordanian Era

Jordan's acquisition of the West Bank as a result of the 1947–49 Palestine war and the 1949 Israel-Jordanian Armistice Agreement marked the beginning of its separate existence as both a geographic and political unit. King Abdullah's Arab Legion initially took control of the West Bank during May 1948, assisted by Egyptian forces in the south and Iraqi troops in the north. As the Arabs were pushed back by the Israelis, the population of the hill country in Judea and Samaria, some 450,000 (including Arab Jerusalem), was swollen by 350,000 of the more than 700,000 refugees from the coastal plain, Galilee and the Negev.

Because of the war and the turmoil following it, no reliable population figures were available for the West Bank until 1952 when the Jordanian authorities gave a total of 742,289, distributed in the following districts: Jerusalem including Arab Jerusalem, Ramallah, and Jericho—301,402; Nablus—315,236; Hebron—125,651. Of these 363,689 were refugees from Israeli-held territory. The refugee population in 1952 was distributed as follows: Nablus—117,934; Jericho—76,184; Jerusalem—58,822; Hebron—56,513; Ramallah—55,246. The first official census conducted by Jordan in 1961 showed the following distribution: Jerusalem—339,454; Nablus—333,191; Hebron—117,768. There was relatively little increase in West Bank population between 1952 and 1961 because of continuous migration of young men to Arab and other countries where economic development was beginning at a rapid pace. In the Hebron district, economic conditions led to population decline with internal migration from Hebron to Jerusalem. By 1967 Jordanian government estimates showed a total of 997,000 of whom 278,255 were refugees.[1]

Integration into Jordan

The transformation of the West Bank from an integral part of Palestine to a western province of the Hashemite Kingdom was traumatic. During the mandatory era, the towns and villages of the West Bank had developed close economic, political and social ties with the rest of Arab

Palestine. The communication network, trade and commerce, and political associations were with Arab communities in Haifa, Jaffa, Jerusalem and the other coastal and Galilee Arab settlements, not with Amman and the Hashemite hinterland. As a result of the war and the armistice agreement these patterns were disrupted and the West Bank became an island isolated between Israel and Jordan's East Bank. Commerce between the cities, towns and villages of the West Bank and the Mediterranean coast was severed. Access to Haifa port was lost. Much of the land and employment sources of the Palestinian population lay across the frontier, in enemy territory.

Scores of towns and villages along the new Jordan-Israel frontier were cut off from traditional village lands and fruit groves which had been the basis of their economy. The armistice line sliced through several villages dividing families, lands, and even houses with part in Israel and part in Jordan. Because Jordan and Israel remained at war, despite the armistice, cross-frontier contact was forbidden by officials on both sides. It seemed that the future of the West Bank would be oriented toward Amman, the new capital of the region's inhabitants.

The Jordanian government kept intact many of the administrative and bureaucratic practices and traditions of the mandatory government. The administrative districts were approximately the same, under district commissioners appointed by Jordan. All inhabitants of the region became Jordanian citizens after Abdullah's annexation of the West Bank, although West Bank Palestinians received easily identifiable passports under Article I of Jordan's constitution. Civil rule replaced military government early in 1949; four Palestinians were added to the cabinet, one of whom was made minister for refugee affairs and deputy governor of Arab Palestine. A year later, all Palestinians in Jordan, including those in the West Bank were invited to vote in national elections, and a new eleven-member cabinet included five Palestinians. In December 1949 King Abdullah let the governorship of Palestine lapse and terminated separate administration on the West Bank. All government business was thereafter conducted from Amman by the respective ministries. Despite protests of the Arab League against the increase of measures pointing toward annexation, Abdullah appointed a new twenty-member House of Notables in April, seven of them Palestinians. A new Chamber of Deputies was also elected, with 20 members from the West Bank and 20 from the East. In a joint session during April 1950 both chambers adopted a resolution supporting "complete unity between the two sides of the Jordan and their union into one state, which is the Hashemite Kingdom of Jordan, at whose head reigns King Abdullah Ibn al Husain, on a basis of constitutional representative government and equality of rights and duties of all citizens."[2]

Annexing West Bank territory and population converted Transjordan from a desert principality under an Emir, into a full-fledged kingdom. As a result of the 1947-49 war there were now nearly half a million Palestine refugees in the country, some 360,000 in the West Bank, 140,000 in the East, in addition to the nearly 400,000 West Bank Palestinians. While two thirds of the new kingdom's total population was Palestinian, centered in western Jordan, 94 percent of the territory was on the east side of the Jordan River.

Great economic and social differences separated the Palestinian majority from the indigenous Jordanians. Nearly twice as many school-aged Palestinian children (52 percent) had been receiving education before the war. Twice as many Palestine Arabs (between 30 and 40 percent) were urbanized. On the other hand, Jordan's four towns with a population of over 10,000 hardly seemed more than a number of adjoining villages. Many of the Palestinians were formerly employed in industry. Over 25,000 had been organized in more than thirty unions. At least half had some contact with nonagricultural occupations. Only the handful of Jordanians who worked for the Iraq Petroleum company or in British military camps did not live from agriculture. The Palestinians were a volatile and politically conscious people, but their fellow Jordanians, except for a few wealthy land owners and merchants, had no political sophistication at all. The nomads on the east side of the Jordan river were quite ignorant of the world beyond and regarded Amman as the ultimate symbol of progress. The Jordanians had become a relatively manageable population as a result of the efforts of the Arab Legion; the Palestinians were a bitter, impoverished, seething body politic, awaiting vengeance for the loss of their homes and land.[3]

Economic Conditions

The bitterness of many Palestinians toward the Jordanian government was exacerbated by the disparity in economic conditions between East and West. Initially the West Bank was economically more advanced although it lost its advantage by the 1960s. Its agricultural output provided 38 percent of Jordan's GNP in 1965 although it covered only 2,300 square miles, 6 percent of the kingdom. Despite mostly rocky soil and irrigation of only 5 percent of the cultivable land, half the West Bank labor force was in agriculture. Produce ranged from wheat, barley, and a variety of vegetables, to grapes, citrus and olives; a third of agricultural output was from livestock. Most irrigation was near Jenin and Jericho. Water scarcity was a major limitation for expanding agriculture (about 35 to 40 percent of the total West Bank was farmed). About 85 percent of the farms were under 25 acres; these smaller farms accounted for about 35 percent of the total cultivated land. About a third of the farmers were tenants.[4]

West Bank industry contributed only 26 percent of Jordan's total GNP, but a much smaller share (6.6 percent) of gross domestic product in the West Bank. By 1965 three quarters of all industrial output was in the East. Existing West Bank industry was small scale: 90 percent of the plants employed less than 10 workers who processed mostly primary goods—food, beverages, tobacco, textiles. Factories also produced furniture, shoes, soap, matches, and traditional craft items such as glassware (Hebron), carpets, embroidery and olive presses. Stone quarrying and construction also contributed to output and employment.[5]

The Jordanian government explicitly favored the East Bank in industrial and infrastructural (electricity, transport) development. This was evident in the location of large semigovernmental projects: only the Jordanian Vegetable Oils Corporation and a match factory were located in Nablus; other major projects including an oil refinery, potash plant and cement factory were placed on the East Bank. Businessmen were compelled to open new factories on the East Bank and sometimes to even transfer businesses there. The only major water development projects, the Yarmuk River dam and the east Ghor Canal, were located in the East. Plans for an extension of the Ghor Canal to the West side of the river were aborted because of the 1967 war. Jordanian authorities argued that large-scale development of industry would have demanded extensive quantities of water which were not available, and that placement of major investments on the West Bank was risky because of the Israeli threat.

Overall, the Jordanian economy grew from 8 to 10 percent annually, with reasonable rates of increase in both agriculture and industry. Per capita annual income increased from $90 in 1950 to about $220 in 1965. Despite the relatively large growth rates, unemployment was high in the West Bank and there was underemployment in agriculture.[6] By 1961 West Bank per capita income was only half that in the East. Care of the large refugee population became a major source of employment. UNRWA not only supported the Jordanian balance of payments, but was one of the largest employers, suppliers and distributors in Jordan.

West Bank economic conditions and the preferential treatment shown for the East, caused a high emigration, both to the East Bank and to the Gulf. Despite a high rate of natural population growth, close to three percent, after nearly eighteen years of Jordanian rule the population only grew by about a third, when it might have been expected to double. Outward migration persisted even after the Jordanian economy as a whole began its rapid development. Most migration was to the East Bank, but by the early 1950s many began the trek to the oil states, especially to Kuwait. Initially the migrants were professionals, skilled and semiskilled workers. Later the less skilled followed as labor shortages developed at the bottom of the wage scale. Remittances sent by the emigrants to families in the West Bank provided a significant proportion of their total income.

Regional Differences[7]

Within the West Bank there were considerable regional differences in patterns of development, migration, and reaction to the policies of the Jordanian government. Hebron, traditionally a conservative Muslim stronghold, had a population with lower skills and education. In 1961 more than 75 percent of its population over 15 had less than four years of formal schooling, a rate about 5 percent more than the West Bank as a whole. Less than a quarter of the population was literate compared to more than a third elsewhere. Outside the city almost 90 percent of the population in the Hebron district lacked a primary education. Other measures of undevelopment were the low level of agricultural technology and the presence of only one physician for each 10,600 inhabitants, compared to one for some 3,700 in Jerusalem District and 7,500 in the Nablus District. The Hebron region was almost totally dependent on agriculture, lacking the variety of other economic sectors in the Jerusalem and Nablus regions. Consequently, migration from the Hebron region was higher than elsewhere in the West Bank. Between 1952 and 1962 there was an overall net migration of 20 percent from the West to the East Bank, but the rate was over 33 percent from Hebron to the East. The rate of migration to the East Bank from Nablus was over 23 percent and almost none from Jerusalem. Hebron's rate of population growth was less than in other regions—4.9 percent compared to 8.4 percent in Nablus and 14.2 percent in Jerusalem.

The Jerusalem District, including the city and its surrounding villages was the most developed. It had the highest rates of schooling and literacy, and its rural population received more formal education. About 70 percent were wage earners, many in handicrafts, compared to only 50 percent in Nablus and Hebron. The percentage in agriculture was lower than in the rest of the West Bank. More than half of all West Bank industry was in the Jerusalem-Ramallah region while less than 10 percent was in the Hebron District.

The Nablus region was the most productive in agriculture, with the largest proportion of rural population—about three quarters. It also had the highest rainfall and richest soil. Farmers in the villages around Nablus, Tulkarm, and Jenin had crop yields that were often twice those in the Jerusalem-Ramallah region. The town of Nablus had the highest percentage of workers in industry—more than a quarter in 1961. Out-migration from the Nablus district was less than from Hebron to other parts of the Middle East, and less than from Jerusalem-Ramallah to the West. Those who did travel were more likely to obtain higher education than the travelers from Hebron and were more likely to return than those from Jerusalem-Ramallah. As it had been since Ottoman times, Nablus remained the center of political and social development, the chief West Bank competition with Jerusalem.

West Bank–Amman Relations[8]

A variety of circumstances contributed to the feelings of deprivation felt by many Palestinians in the West Bank and to their sense of alienation against the Hashemite regime in Amman. On the one hand, the Palestinians realized that their levels of political and social development were far more advanced than those of the indigenous beduin inhabitants of the East. On the other hand, Jordanian government policies strongly favored the economic development of the eastern part of the kingdom, despite the West Bank's superior abilities and human resources. Initial attempts by the Hashemite regime to equalize political representation between East and West in the newly created political institutions of Jordan were subverted by the favoritism shown to the Transjordanian intimates of the king and the suspicion against Palestinians revealed by their exclusion from the most sensitive posts in the army, police, security apparatus, and in the royal palace. For example, between 1953 and 1956 seven of the Arab Legion's eighteen regiments were composed overwhelmingly of beduins. Most recruits from the West Bank served as technicians, and those who were in infantry regiments were usually not combat soldiers. The key positions, and those in most elite combat corps were given to East Bank "loyalists."

King Abdullah attempted to reward Palestinian leaders with whom he had formed alliances during the mandatory period. At the local level he tried to coopt members of municipal councils and to influence elections for local offices. Several Palestinians were appointed as provincial governors, as members of the Israel-Jordan Mixed Armistice Commission, as representatives for refugee affairs, and in senior posts related to education and economics. Such appointments were generally to notables with high social standing, often to support cooperative candidates in local and national elections. Many of the appointees had backed Abdullah's aspiration to become king of Palestine during the Mandate and had helped engineer support for annexation among the Palestinians. The most important of these notables were members of the Nashashibi clan or individuals who had worked closely with the

Nashashibis during the Mandate. In the period immediately after annexation, five of the eight West Bankers appointed to the Senate (House of Notables) were Nashashibis. Two others were associated with the clan, and only one of the eight, Abd al-Latif Salah, did not belong to the Nashashibi political group. Salah, however, had been an open opponent of the Husaynis for many years.

Other appointments were used by Abdullah to placate former opponents and to coopt them. A Ba'athist leader, Khulusi Kheyri, was persuaded to join the government in 1952 and served as minister of economics and development in six of the next ten cabinets. Anwar Nuseibeh, a Husayni, and secretary of the competing All-Palestine Government set up under Egypt in Gaza by the opponents of Abdullah, served in several high Jordanian posts after 1952.

Many West Bank Palestinians granted King Abdullah "conditional legitimacy" allowing them to accept affiliation with the Hashemite regime, while maintaining their ultimate objective of liberation. Others felt that compromise with Jordan was necessary for practical reasons, to gain citizenship, to acquire a passport, to obtain commercial licenses, employment, education and social services. In time many areas of Jordan's life and administration at all levels of the educational, economic, and political system came to be dominated by Palestinians.

At the upper levels, the old strife between the Councilite followers of the Mufti, Haj Amin al-Husayni, and the Nashashibi Opposition was reflected in competition between the Egyptian-backed All-Palestine Government, set up in Gaza during 1948, and the Palestine Congresses organized under Abdullah's tutelage in Amman and Jericho during 1948-49. Each faction claimed to be the true heir of Palestinian Arab nationalism, although each was controlled by a non-Palestinian Arab government. The Gaza All-Palestine Government had little authority, few accomplishments, and withered away, without even the formality of an official decree. The Palestinian Congresses, in effect, voted themselves out of existence when they proclaimed the unification of East and West Jordan, and recognized Emir Abdullah as the leader of the new Hashemite Kingdom.

Not all West Bank Palestinians supported annexation or the Nashashibis, nor were all Palestinians in Gaza Mufti enthusiasts. Several members of the Gaza All-Palestinian faction later joined Abdullah's administration, even though Jordan never controlled Gaza. His most notable supporter in Gaza was Rashad Shawa, who was to become mayor of the city. Generally speaking, however, the Mufti's radical pan-Arab politics appealed to the refugee population in both Gaza, the East and West Banks, whereas the "moderate" pro-Jordanian trend found most of its support among nonrefugees, including independent farmers, land owners, businessmen and professionals who were interested in political stability, a predictable government administration, and laying foundations for secure economic development. In general terms, and with some exceptions, these trends, the radical pan-Arab and moderate pro-Jordanian, were later to become absorbed in moderate and radical expressions of West Bank political support for the various Palestinian political factions, i.e., those favoring some kind of compromise with Israel, and those that opposed any negotiations with or concessions to the Jewish state.

Refugee-Nonrefugee Tensions[9]

The tension between refugees and nonrefugees was much exacerbated by the situation along Israel's frontiers, where thousands of the former were sheltered in camps and villages. Only a third of the refugee population was in camps; the rest were initially sheltered in village mosques, schools, or other public buildings. Later many were absorbed by relatives, or in installations provided by the Jordan government. Even in ordinary times it would have been difficult for frontier towns like Qalqilya and Tulkarm to absorb hundreds or thousands of refugees, but after the 1948 war, with so much of their productive lands now on the Israeli side of the border economic conditions became particularly difficult.

The influx of refugees only made things worse. The refugees squatted on local land, and appropriated crops and scarce water, arousing the ire of the villagers. Frequently they were abused and reminded that "a guest is not forever welcome." In many areas the refugees were exploited by the farmers, paid low wages, and charged extortionate rents. More serious was the danger posed to the frontier villages by refugee infiltration across the border into Israel. The Israelis held the West Bank villages accountable and often made them the victims of retaliation. As infiltration became more aggressive, the incidence and severity of Israeli retaliation increased. The whole frontier was destabilized by this destructive cycle. The villagers turned against not only the refugees but also the Jordanian government because of its failure to protect them. The government responded by establishing a National Guard to ward off, delay or even stop the Israeli attacks. Until its amalgamation into the Jordanian army in 1965, the Palestine National Guard was not very effective. Consisting mostly of villagers garrisoned in their own homes, the Guard had limited supplies, weapons and mobility. Furthermore, the Jordanian army commanders were reluctant to see the force become too strong lest it become a tool in the hands of the many dissidents opposed to the monarchy. The government became especially leery of placing military material in the hands of a semiautonomous Palestine force after the widespread protests against the King following the Israeli raids on Qibya in 1953 and es-Samu in 1966.

Inter-Arab Politics

Political developments in the West Bank during Jordanian rule were overshadowed by the turmoil and radical changes occurring in the broader Arab world. The overthrow of monarchies in Egypt during 1952 and Iraq in 1958, the rise of Nasser as the dominant figure in the Middle East, nationalization of the Suez Canal and Czech supply of arms to Egypt, the war in Yemen, the ascent of the Ba'ath party in Syria, civil war in Lebanon during 1958, all profoundly affected political perspectives in the West Bank and in Jordan. Because their own political leaders had been discredited as a result of Arab failures in the 1948 war, many Palestinians turned to leaders and movements such as Nasser, the Ba'ath, the Communists, and the Muslim Brothers. Nasser was the most influential, because he was the most charismatic and understood more than others the aspirations of the Arab middle class as well as the masses.

By the 1960s Nasser's picture hung beside the King's in thousands of West Bank homes and schools, in refugee camps and in towns and villages. He, more than others, seemed capable of avenging Palestinian and Arab disgrace, of restoring the refugees to their homes and of eliminating the Israeli threat. Events in the Arab world, especially the rise of Nasser, radicalized West Bank politics and even forced the Jordanian monarchy to adopt many measures and reforms contrary to its conservative inclinations. One of the most dramatic moves was King Hussein's response to formation of the United Arab Republic in 1958, an event that stirred tremendous enthusiasm in all parts of the Arab world, although it also aroused apprehension in many Arab governments. The King's reaction was to form the Hashemite Arab Union with Iraq, but it aroused none of the enthusiasm that greeted the UAR. The Hashemite Union was aborted a few weeks later by the July 1958 revolution that overthrew Iraq's monarchy.

Events in the Arab world had their greatest impact within Jordan and the West Bank between 1956 and 1958, following the election of the National Socialists, a pro-Nasser, anti-Western party led by Sulaiman Nabulsi which won eleven of the forty seats in parliament. Election of the Nabulsi government followed a period of country-wide political unrest and demonstrations, partly in support of Nasser's nationalization of the Suez Canal, partly in protest against what many Palestinians perceived to be King Hussein's anti-nationalist and conservative policies.

The October 1956 elections, the fourth in Jordan's history, were the first, and probably only ones, which were relatively free and unhindered. In addition to Nabulsi's pro-Egyptian National Socialists, the Communist-supported National Front won three seats, and the Ba'athists, two. The Muslim Brotherhood, radicals at the other end of the spectrum, won four seats. Election of the Nabulsi government led to the reorientation of Jordan's foreign policy and ultimately to the dismissal of General John B. Glubb and other British officers from Jordan's army. But the policy reversal was short-lived. Within a few months the new government's radical policies so frightened the King and his entourage, that he dismissed Nabulsi in April 1957, had the army arrest some 500 leftist and Communist politicians, and outlawed several of the more radical parties.

The West Bank was the center of most anti-establishment political activity and the home of most dissident political leaders. It provided the popular support for the banned parties. Even after leftist groups were banned, several of them continued to operate secretly in the West Bank. Although small in numbers the most important was the Communist Party, which maintained its underground existence when Israel took over after 1967.

There was no revival of a distinctive Palestinian political identity until 1964. In January 1964 the Arab League decided to establish the Palestine Liberation Organization, whose founding congress was held in Jerusalem in May. Jordan permitted West Bank mayors and the Palestinian representatives in parliament (no longer elected but appointed) to attend. Because the new organization threatened Jordan's effort to make Jordanians of the Palestinians, considerable tension developed between the small PLO office in Jerusalem and Jordanian officials.

The creation of the PLO coincided with growth of the more militant Fatah, led by Yasir Arafat, with headquarters in Damascus. Despite Jordan's ban on Fatah, its very first guerrilla operation involved a raid across Jordanian territory into Israel on January 1, 1965. Israel's retaliation against Jordan for this and other guerrilla activities precipitated public demonstrations against the regime and new demands for arms and military action against Israel.

Although Nasser still dominated the political scene, the newly formed PLO and the guerrilla activities of Fatah now gave the West Bank Palestinians a force of their own with which to identify. The Nasserite slogan of "unity, liberation and revenge," evoked more support and hope than the still marginal activities of the new Palestinian groups. Belief prevailed that Palestine could be liberated only through a strong and united Arab world. Thus the great excitement that swept the West

Bank and the rest of the Arab world after establishment of the UAR in 1958.

By 1967 Nasser generated enthusiasm throughout the Arab world for a new round of battle with Israel and he mobilized support from Syria and Jordan in a unified Arab command to be headed by an Egyptian general. By May 1967 Arab public opinion was primed for the third round; there were mass demonstrations in Arab Jerusalem and in the West Bank urging King Hussein to join the oncoming war.

Israel's preemptive attack on Egypt, Syria, and Iraq wiped out their Air Forces on June 4–5, 1967, subjecting King Hussein to great public pressure to join the fray. Despite warnings from Israel against any precipitous military action, Jordan opened fire from Jerusalem, leading to its eventual defeat, along with Egypt and Syria, and loss of the whole West Bank after only three days of combat. The loss of West Bank resulted in a major escalation of the Arab refugee problem and the total transformation of the demographic, political and economic face of the West Bank. The West Bank was now placed under its fourth political regime within fifty years.

Major Trends and Developments, 1900–1967

(1) From 1900 until 1918 Palestine was part of the declining Ottoman Empire. Despite the Ottoman collapse in 1918, four hundred years of Turkish rule left distinctive imprints which remained in the law and administration of the country, especially in the land system, in the social organization of the Arab community, and in its Islamic hierarchy.

(2) Palestinian Arab nationalism emerged by the early 1920s as a movement affiliated with the broader movements of Arab nationalism, yet, as a result of the particular circumstances of the British Mandate and the rivalry with Zionist nationalism in the country, a separate Palestinian identity developed with its own political goals and aspirations.

(3) After World War I the Jewish community in Palestine increased from less than a tenth to a third of the population, with substantial economic and political institutions, later to become the foundation upon which the State of Israel was established. The growth of this community led to civil strife during the Mandate between Palestine's Arabs and Jews over questions of Jewish immigration, Jewish land acquisition, and political control of the country.

(4) British attempts during the Mandate to mediate the differences between Jewish and Palestinian nationalism failed, despite British introduction of a modern bureaucracy, attempted political self-government, and relatively modern economic and social institutions.

(5) During the Mandate the Palestinian Arab community experienced economic and demographic growth at a relatively rapid rate in comparison to the surrounding Arab countries, but at a much slower rate than the growth of the Palestinian Jewish community. Thus the Arab community was relatively "underdeveloped" in relation to the Jewish community.

(6) By the end of World War II the Mandate collapsed, first as a result of civil war between Jews and Arabs and British, then as a result of the war between the new Jewish State and the surrounding Arab countries. This resulted in division of the country into the State of Israel, the Egyptian-occupied Gaza Strip, and the Jordanian-annexed West Bank.

(7) Jordanian attempts to integrate the West Bank into the Hashemite Kingdom failed because of the existence of a distinctive Palestinian Arab identity, the reluctance of the Hashemite rulers to fully trust the Palestinians, and the influence of wider political trends in the Arab world which affected the population in the West Bank. These influences included Nasserism, and radical movements such as the Ba'ath, and Communism.

(8) Under Jordanian rule there was continued economic retardation in the West Bank because of its lack of resources, Jordanian economic policies, and the large refugee influx from the 1947-48 war with Israel.

Notes

1. Bassam Abed, "Demographic Profile of Palestine 1900–1983."op.cit.

2. Benjamin Schwadran, *Jordan A State of Tension*, New York, 1959,p. 249.

3. Don Peretz, *The Middle East Today*, 4th edition, New York, 1983, p. 347.

4. Arie Bregman, *Economic Growth in the Administered Areas, 1968–1973*, Jerusalem, 1975, pp. 47, 39, 52; Vivian Bull, *The West Bank—Is it Viable?*, Lexington, Mass., 1975, p. 64; Brian Van Arkadie, *Benefits and Burdens: A Report on the West Bank and Gaza Strip Economics since 1967*, New York and Washington, 1977, pp. 22, 24, 27.

5. Ibid., Bregman, pp. 4, 47, 63; Bull, pp. 95, 96; Van Arkadie, p. 23.

6. Ibid., Bregman, pp. 6, 9–11, 14; Van Arkadie, pp. 22–24.

7. Joel S. Migdal, *Palestinian Society and Politics*, pp. 56–60.

8. See Amnon Cohen, *Political Parties in the West Bank Under the Jordanian Regime, 1949–1967*, Ithaca, 1982; Shaul Mishal, *West Bank/East Bank: The Palestinians in Jordan, 1949–1967*, New Haven, 1978; Mishal, *"Conflictual Pressures and Cooperative Interests: Observations on West Bank–Amman Political Relations, 1949–1967,"* in Migdal 1980; Avi Plascov, *The Palestinian Refugees in Jordan 1948-57*, London, 1981; Benjamin Schwadran, *Jordan A State of Tension*, 1959, Chapter XV, "Annexation of Arab Palestine."

9. Ibid., Avi Plascov.

Part 2
The West Bank Under Israeli Occupation, 1967 and After

Israel's occupation of the West Bank since 1967 has caused changes as far-reaching and traumatic as those caused by the severance of the area from the rest of mandatory Palestine during the 1947-49 war. Although the territorial unity of mandatory Palestine (without Jordan) was restored in 1967 under Israeli rule, the political, economic, social and demographic impact of Israeli occupation since 1967 has been more pervasive than the changes resulting from the pre-1967 period. The consequences of the occupation have affected not only the West Bank itself, but Jordan and Israel as well.

Key issues that have arisen during the nearly 20 years of Israeli occupation are:

(1) Will Israel remain in the West Bank, and if it does remain, what will be the status of the territory and of its population under Israeli jurisdiction? What will the situation of the West Bank be if it is returned to Jordan or if it attains independence, autonomy, or some other political status?

(2) What has been the pattern of Israeli policies within the West Bank in relation to the local Arab population, to public administration, and to the economic and social organization of the area? How have the patterns differed under the Labor and Likud governments?

(3) How large and how important has Jewish settlement been in the West Bank, and how has it affected the Arab population of the area, political developments within Israel, and Israel's foreign relations, especially with the U.S., Jordan, Egypt, and other Arab countries?

(4) What political and social trends have emerged among the local West Bank Arab population and to what extent are they a continuation of trends established since 1900 under Ottoman, British, and Jordanian rule? How has the economic and social development of the West Bank Arab population been affected by Israel's occupation since 1967?

(5) How have developments in the West Bank since 1967 affected the wider scope of Middle East politics and American Middle East policy options?

4

The Israeli Dimension

Israeli Policies Under Labor

During the first weeks after the 1967 war Foreign Minister Abba Eban declared that the June 5th map of the region had been "destroyed irrevocably," but that Israel was prepared to negotiate new frontiers with its Arab neighbors. Jerusalem was an exception not subject to negotiation. Within a month after the cease-fire the city was incorporated into the Israeli West Jerusalem municipality. Not only the Arab Old City and Jordanian municipality of East Jerusalem, but an area of the West Bank between Bethlehem and Ramallah, including Kalandia airport and several Arab villages, were absorbed within the newly extended borders of Israel's capital. The approximately 65,000 Arab inhabitants in this "greater Jerusalem" (now over 120,000) were considered residents of Israel.[1] They were entitled to vote in municipal elections, but were also permitted to retain Jordanian passports, and were thus ineligible to vote in Israel's national elections. Very few Arabs took advantage of the offer to become naturalized Israeli citizens.

From the start of Israel's occupation the future of the West Bank was a subject of controversy both within the government and among the public. From an Israeli perspective the region was at least as important as territory controlled before the June war, if not more so. It was an integral part of historic Eretz Israel containing some of the sites most revered in Jewish tradition such as the Tomb of Rachel in Bethlehem and the Tomb of the Prophets at Hebron. Even the Labor movement called the West Bank, "Eretz Israel" and many of its members regretted that the borders had not been extended to include the region during the 1948 war. Toward the end of that war several commanders had urged Ben Gurion to seize the West Bank from Jordan, but he refused, fearing British intervention should Jordan's Arab Legion be defeated. He indicated, however, that opportunities for liberation of the West Bank would surely present themselves in the future.

Only Menacheem Begin's irredentist Herut party openly claimed the West Bank between 1948 and 1967, claiming as well the Hashemite

Kingdom of Jordan, which had been part of the original Mandate. Within the armed forces certain "activist" officers pressed for measures that might precipitate Israel's occupation of the West Bank.[2] Harsh retaliation raids were mounted against Arab border villages, aimed at creating an environment favorable to Israel's seizure of the West Bank.

Pressures to maintain Israel's hold on the occupied territories were renewed after 1967, following the Arab failure to accept an offer for direct peace negotiations. Small but increasing numbers of religiously oriented Jews joined the irredentists in pressuring the government to adopt the "liberation" of Judea and Samaria as official policy, to encourage settlement by Jews and ultimately, to incorporate the West Bank into the Jewish state. By the seventh Knesset election in 1968 public opinion had moved far from acceptance of the pre-1967 status quo, toward the Herut position. Begin's stance was clear, unambiguous, and thus attractive, while the Labor Alignment, a coalition of center and leftist labor parties, was factionalized among diverse approaches toward the Occupied Territories. The left wing Mapam faction, for example, with its origins in the Kibbutz movements, had a policy of quasi-withdrawal or "peace without territories." Other factions voiced greater reservations about the need for withdrawal. Since the Alignment represented a spectrum of views the result was internal polarization, and the erosion of public support.

The necessity of governing through coalitions was another factor behind the ambiguity of the Labor government's policies. The presence of the National Religious Party (NRP) in the Alignment's coalition was a key source of discord. Without the NRP the Alignment-led government would have been unable to maintain its Knesset majority. The leaders of Labor were thus forced to make a number of compromises with the religious party.

Defense Minister Moshe Dayan made an attempt to reconcile these diverse views in his doctrine of "new facts," emphasizing that Israel was in the West Bank "of right and not on sufferance, to visit, live and to settle . . . we must be able to maintain military bases there . . . we must of course, be able to prevent the entry of any Arab army into the West Bank." Arabs living there, Dayan stated, would not be forced to become Israelis, but should be permitted to retain Jordanian citizenship while living in Israeli-controlled enclaves.[3]

Under the "new facts" policy Jewish settlements were organized according to a plan proposed by Deputy Prime Minister Yigal Allon, but never officially adopted because of divisions within the government. It envisaged a ring of Jewish settlements around the Arab-inhabited areas of the West Bank, with Jenin, Nablus and Ramallah as their center. In the Hebron area permission was given for reestablishment of

Jewish settlements on the strategic site of the former Etzion Bloc abandoned by Jewish settlers during the 1948 war. The basic concept of the Allon plan was to permit the Arab population to govern itself, with as little interference as possible from Israel, but to leave all strategic points in the West Bank under Israeli military control.[4]

Establishing "new facts" necessitated a major extension of the road network, setting up scores of military bases and outposts and organizing Israeli business and commercial operations in the Occupied Territories. In pursuit of these objectives, the Labor government encouraged Jewish investors and gave them assistance. Benefits included cheaper prices for raw materials, lower interest rates on loans, government sureties in regard to security and tax relief under the law to encourage investment. Special subsidies were offered to nonresidents who could find partners among West Bank inhabitants. Long-term policies required Israeli investment in the West Bank, according to Dayan.

The Defense Minister's "new facts" doctrine did not go unchallenged. It was openly opposed by Finance Minister Pinhas Sapir who expressed apprehension about growing dependence on unskilled and semi-skilled Arab labor from the territories. While numbering only five percent of Israel's total work force, twenty percent of the workers in such vital sectors as construction and agriculture were Arab by 1969. Even left wing kibbutzim used Arab labor for less desirable farm jobs, menial factory chores and cleaning details. Arabs were displacing the Oriental Jews who were moving up in the social ladder.

Neither the allure of higher wages, nor better working conditions and social services, would diminish anti-Zionism or the growth of militant nationalism among Arab laborers from the territories, Sapir warned. Should the country be faced with economic recession, nearly a quarter of the work force, according to Sapir, would become embittered: they would be the first to lose their jobs. To preserve Israel as the Jewish state, he warned, it would be necessary to not only maintain political separation, but to sever the economic bonds that were rapidly binding the two peoples together. Dayan's "open bridges" program, which permitted Arabs to move relatively freely across the Jordan River, was not regarded as a boon by Sapir. Rather, he perceived it as an opening wedge to "dezionisation." Eventually Sapir softened his opposition to Dayan's program, out of loyalty to the party and to Prime Minister Golda Meir.[5]

Ambiguity and indecisiveness within the Labor leadership continued through the eighth Knesset election in 1973, when the Alignment proposed a four-year scheme for the West Bank called the Galili plan. It reiterated programs for extensive investment in West Bank infrastructure and assistance to Israeli business, providing for an industrial zone in Qalqilya and Tulkarm. The Israel Land Authority was empowered to "step in [and] acquire land and real estate in the territories for the purposes of settlement, development and land exchanges . . . through every effective means." A long debate over private acquisition of Arab lands and property in the occupied areas was resolved by establishing a special cabinet committee empowered to grant permits "on condition that the purchases are transacted for the purpose of constructive projects and not for speculative purposes, and within the framework of government policy."[6]

By election time in December 1973, Labor had modified the Galili document. It toned down the more explicit references to Israel's role in the occupied territories and omitted mention of large investments or acquisition of land by either government or private sources. Instead, the new program focused on Israel's position until peace treaties or interim arrangements could be concluded. During this period, "Israel will continue to maintain the situation as determined at the time, with priority for security considerations." Although the new program called for territorial compromise, it warned that "Israel will not return to the lines of June 4, 1967, which were a temptation to aggression."[7]

Following the election it remained unclear whether or not the Galili plan still represented Labor's position. Sapir insisted that it had been "repealed," Dayan said that it had not. The party's secretary general asserted that a new program simply "overlay" the previous one. Mapam viewed the new "Sapir document," in contrast to the more hawkish Galili plan, as a "truly dovish platform . . . Mapam considered the new platform to have cancelled out both the Galili Document and oral doctrines associated with Defense Minister Moshe Dayan."[8]

Further, the Zionist bureaucracy and institutions established before 1948 to build the Jewish state and to settle the land, including the Jewish National Fund (land acquisition and development), the Jewish Agency (immigrant absorption and settlement construction), and various cooperative and collective settlement (kibbutz) federations, saw in the occupied territories new vistas for expanding their activities in areas closed to them prior to the 1967 war. Acquisition of the new territories revived the pioneering zeal, the challenge, and the ideal of sacrifice that had infused these institutions before 1948. These organizations, then, constituted ready-made instrumentalities as well as a strong pressure group for reactivation of traditional Zionist programs for settlement and absorption of the West Bank, regardless of the political objectives of the Labor leadership.

Ambiguity in policy toward the West Bank arising from these diverse internal factors was reinforced by the refusal of the Arab states to negotiate a peace settlement with Israel. The intransigence of the PLO made it doubly difficult for Israelis inclined to preserve options for disengagement from the West Bank to convince others to abandon the idea of annexation.

Overarching all these incentives to refrain from formulating a decisive policy was the gradual erosion of Labor's ideological commitments and the loss of the idealism that characterized the movement before the state was established and in its early history. After dominating the Zionist movement and the Yishuv for more than 40 years the Labor party had lost its élan. Its leadership was tired and aging. Seriously divided by personal power struggles, Labor suffered from corruption and the image of arrogant Ashkenazi disregard for the Oriental communities who, by the late 1960s, had become the majority of the population.

The Renewal of Nationalism

The ambiguities in Labor's programs and policies encouraged militant Jewish nationalists who were eager to push the policy makers toward full integration, if not actual legal annexation, of the West Bank into Israel. *The Whole Land of Israel Movement* was founded after the 1967 war by "activists" in the Labor Party and right-wing intellectuals to serve as an ideological and elite-oriented pressure group toward annexation of all territories occupied during the war.

Another militant nationalist group, called *Gush Emunim* (Block of the Faithful), was formed after the 1973 war, when debate over the future of the West Bank intensified. It was formally founded at a conference of Yeshiva students in February 1974 for the purpose of forcing the government's hand. Gush Emunim has emphasized mobilization of popular energies to create new facts in the occupied territories binding future governments to its vision of the entire Land of Israel under permanent Jewish sovereignty. Since 1974 Gush Emunim has attracted followers from nonreligious, nationalist groups, like the Whole Land of Israel Movement, many of whom have joined its settlements. In this period, Gush Emunim sought to nullify the Allon plan by establishing settlements, without government authorization, in areas that were to be returned to Arab control. In December 1975, after repeated unsuccessful attempts to establish a settlement in the Nablus area, Gush settlers set up a quasi settlement at the ancient site of Sebastiya. Deterred from ordering the army to evict the settlers because of effective Gush lobbying, Prime Minister Rabin agreed that the Sebastiya settlers would "voluntarily" evacuate themselves to an army camp at Kaddum, nearby. (The encampment was transformed to a "legal" civilian settlement by the Begin government in 1977.)

Thousands of members of the NRP's youth movement, Bnei Akiva, along with students in army-affiliated religious seminaries known as Yeshivot Hesder, formed the political base for Gush Emunim and its annexationist policies. Leaders of the Religious Youth Movement held the balance of power in the NRP, and threatened to leave the coalition should Labor's West Bank policies block their goal of integrating Judea and Samaria into the Jewish state. They were associated with the recently deceased Rabbi Zvi Yehuda Kook, son of Israel's first Chief Rabbi, Abraham Kook. Rabbi Zvi Kook was regarded as a contemporary sage and major critic of Israel's establishment from an orthodox Jewish perspective. Israel's leaders, he asserted, had betrayed their holy mission by permitting the deterioration of Jewish values internally and compromising the nation's historical destiny through territorial concessions.[9]

Gush Emunim was an important partner of the World Zionist Organization in promotion of Jewish immigration to Israel, especially to the West Bank. It has had moderate success with recruitment of American Jews who now constitute a sizable proportion of the organization's members and of settlers in the West Bank. While most of its supporters are from the Ashkenazi middle class, Gush Emunim strives to reach the Oriental lower class without much success. It has demonstrated its political clout through the organization of mass demonstrations and as a counterforce to Peace Now, a movement opposed to Jewish settlement in the West Bank. Gush Emunim has not yet endorsed a particular political party or offered its own list of Knesset candidates. However, it has sympathizers or supporters among Knesset members from the NRP, Likud, Tehiya and Morasha. The core of its membership is represented by 10,000 West Bank settlers. Its small staff coordinates activities of diverse groups and organizations which have formed within it and on its fringes. They have included *Amana,* a body specializing in organization and establishment of settlements; the fund for Land Redemption, created to expand Jewish ownership of land in the West Bank through purchase; and Residential Quarters, in Judea and Samaria, created by Tehiya for the same reason. The secular leadership of Gush Emunim has provided several leaders of Tehiya. There has been some suspicion and growing evidence, that Gush Emunim settlers (if not the organization itself) have ties with Jewish extremists who use violence against West Bank Arabs and against Israeli Jews active in the peace movement.

*   *   *

The Labor government's principal objectives seemed to be (1) maintenance of the status quo, with emphasis on security, under conservative local leadership supervised by Israel; (2) economic integration of the West Bank with Israel through the use of Arab labor, the marketing of Israeli products in the West Bank and of noncompetitive West Bank primary products in Israel, and the linking of West Bank infrastructure with Israel; (3) using the West Bank as an opening wedge to the Arab world, through Dayan's "Open Bridges" policy, facilitating visits from Arab countries of "trustworthy" visitors and through export of products from Israel across the bridges to Jordan, and from Jordan to other Arab countries; (4) establishment of Jewish settlements in selected areas as security outposts.

By the time of Sadat's visit to Jerusalem in 1977 and the negotiations over the future of the West Bank following the 1979 peace treaty with Egypt, Labor had been displaced by a new coalition for the first time in the history of the state. Menachem Begin and his Herut party dominated the new government coalition. It was as unambiguous and as decisive in its commitment to incorporate the West Bank into Israel as the previous Labor governments under Eshkol, Meir and Rabin had been vacillating and indecisive.

Although the institutionalization of Israel's presence on the West Bank advanced considerably in the last decade of Labor's rule, this had not been accomplished through the consistent application of a coherent policy. In contrast to the years ahead, the expansion of Israel's role in the West Bank from 1967 to 1977 was marked by indecision and divisiveness among key political figures, and the exploitation of these weaknesses by a determined annexationist minority.

Likud Policies

Neither Menachem Begin nor the Herut movement concealed their ambition to annex the West Bank to Israel. The territorial unity of the "whole Land of Israel" was the basis of their political ideology, and thus not amenable to compromise. Herut and its predecessor, the revisionist Zionist movement founded in the 1930's by Vladimir Jabotinsky, were established on the basis of irredentism, i.e., unification of historical Israel within the borders of the Jewish state. A fundamental objective of the Begin governments of 1977 and 1981 was to eliminate all options for the future of the West Bank except permanent incorporation into Israel. All policy and all decisions related to the West Bank after 1977 were based on this goal.

The awareness by Herut leaders that their commitment to permanent incorporation of the West Bank was not shared by many Israelis, including some in the Likud coalition, led Begin to intensify West Bank settlement activity. Some Likud partisans perceived their new authority as a fleeting opportunity to preempt the future of the West Bank by establishing irrevocable facts before they were removed from power. This led to close cooperation with Gush Emunim in place of the uncertain relations that had existed between the Gush and Labor. The acceleration of Jewish settlement in and near heavily populated Arab sectors of the West Bank was encouraged presumably to nullify possibilities for future implementation of the Allon plan.

Although the future of the West Bank was one of the most crucial issues in the peace negotiations with Egypt, Begin succeeded in avoiding a clear-cut decision through his autonomy scheme presented to the Knesset in December 1977.[10] In this way he was able to circumvent Egyptian and U.S. efforts to formulate a political plan for the region contrary to Likud's goals.[11] Those close to Begin explained that he agreed to the Camp David accords, especially to return of Sinai (to which he had no ideological ties), only because he believed that peace with Egypt would further his goal of a Greater Israel. One interpretation of the Egyptian-Israeli Treaty is that Begin gave up Sinai in exchange for the West Bank.

Begin's policies circumvented the legal restrictions placed by the Supreme Court on Jewish settlement and land acquisition in the West Bank through various administrative devices. These included greatly increasing government subsidization of West Bank settlements, initiating vast West Bank housing projects open to middle class Israelis regardless of political orientation, the intensification of control policies to discourage Palestinian belief in national coexistence with the Jewish state, and promulgation, through Israel's national education system, the media, and the army, of the image of Israel rightfully and necessarily stretching from the Mediterranean Sea to the Jordan River.

An initial thrust of Likud's West Bank program was to undermine the Allon Plan by broadening the area of permissible Jewish settlement from a thin chain of kibbutzim and moshavim running through the Jordan Valley, to the whole West Bank. The number of Jewish settlements was tripled, from 36 to well over 100 by 1983.[12] The number of Jewish settlers increased some sixfold, from nearly 5,000 to more than 30,000 (excluding Jerusalem) during this period. Settlers from Gush Emunim no longer regarded the government as an adversary, but as a partner in achieving its goals. Dayan's policy of "nonintervention" was officially discarded as the armed forces and Military Government establishment became more active in the surveillance and suppression of Arab dissidence, and in assistance to Jewish settlers, especially to Gush Emunim. The pretense of a "neutral" peacekeeping role in controversies between Jews and Arabs was abandoned. This change was underscored by the resignation in May 1980 of Ezer Weizman as Minister of Defense, partially because of disagreements with Begin on West Bank policy. He was replaced by Ariel Sharon, who, with Chief-of-Staff Rafael Eitan, openly advocated annexation and a tough occupation policy. Shortly after his appointment, Eitan, contrary to the precedent banning generals from making political pronouncements, issued a public declaration affirming Israel's right to the West Bank. With the appointment of a Gush Emunim leader as adviser to the army's Chief Education Officer, the IDF's new ideological and political orientation was apparent.

Placement of new settlements during the first two-and-a-half years of the Begin administration underscored the direction of policy. Twenty-nine of the thirty-five settlements established or legalized between 1977 and 1980 were located in areas considered "out of bounds" in the Allon Plan, in the hill country of the northern bulge of the West Bank (Samaria), in the Jericho and Hebron areas.

A 1980 analysis of government expenditures showed that between nine and thirteen percent of Israel's entire development budget was for settlements in the occupied territories. This was exclusive of monies allocated by nongovernmental Zionist institutions. One official of the Jewish Agency's Land Settlement Department reported that the first 21 settlements established in the West Bank under the Begin government cost more than $3 million each. These settlements, he stated, represented little more than a "pegging of stakes into the area." By the end of 1982 the deputy Minister of Agriculture reported that the government operated on the assumption that it cost between $125,000 and $155,000 to settle each family on the West Bank. The Director General of the Ministry of Housing and Construction indicated that his ministry invested $110.4 million in the West Bank during 1982 compared to $141 million in Israeli urban development. Housing Minister David Levi told the Knesset that the Ministry spent over $40 million on West Bank settlement during the 1982-83 fiscal year, twice what it spent in the Negev or the Jordan Valley.[13]

A new dimension of Likud policy was to subsidize investment and residence in the West Bank. These subsidies have persuaded many middle class Israelis who were unable to find affordable living quarters within the major urban centers to move to the West Bank. The subsidized West Bank housing estates were intensively advertised in the media, emphasizing such advantages as "clean air," detached or semidetached villas, relatively short commuting time to coastal metropolitan areas, etc. The government provides rapid transportation links to the coastal plain by-passing Arab towns and villages.[14]

These investments have helped to create a domestic lobby with an economic interest in the West Bank. Although not large relative to Israel's total population, even 100,000 voters constitute the basis of the four or five marginal Knesset seats needed to carry the Likud program forward or to block any territorial compromises. The "Master Plan for Settlement of Samaria and Judea" prepared by the World Zionist Organization and the Israel Ministry of Agriculture in 1983 estimated that there were 100,000 families potentially willing to move into West Bank suburbs during the next decade.

Land already seized by the Israeli government as "state domain" and private lots already purchased are sufficient for construction of hundreds of thousands of residential units. Given the pace of construction prior to formation of the new National Unity Government in September 1984, including infrastructure such as roads, water systems, and electrical facilities, 10,000 to 15,000 more people could be housed in the West Bank each year. The ten-year total amount required for investment was estimated at $1.5 billion to be provided by both public and private sources. This amount represented about ten percent of the American aid expected to be provided to Israel during the same period. Funds were also supplied by private Zionist organizations. In October 1983 mayors of four West Bank towns and others sued in a U.S. federal court to revoke tax exemptions of the UJA and five other Jewish organizations on grounds that they were channeling contributions to Israeli organizations to confiscate land from Palestinians.

Likud's Autonomy Plan

Provisions of the Camp David agreements and the ancillary protocols to the Egyptian-Israeli peace treaty were ambiguous about the future of the West Bank. As a result, each party could interpret them according to its own interests. Prime Minister Begin gave Israel's interpretation of "autonomy" in his 26-point "peace plan" before the Knesset in December 1977.[15] In contrast to the Egyptian and American interpretations of "autonomy" which envisaged eventual self-government for the Palestinians, the Begin plan foresaw integration of the West Bank into Israel; autonomy would apply to the Arab inhabitants but not to the territory. The plan generated controversy among Begin's extremist followers who regarded it as too conciliatory, and became one of the causes for a split in Herut leading to the formation of the more militantly annexationist Tehiya party.

Begin's blueprint was modeled on the concept of "personal autonomy" proposed for Jewish communities in pre-World War I Eastern Europe. He emphasized that "full autonomy" mentioned in the Camp David agreements in no way implied territorial or political separation from Israel. "The Green Line," he stated, "no longer exists—it has vanished forever. There is no line anymore. We want to coexist with the Arabs in Eretz Israel . . . under the autonomy scheme they will run their own internal affairs and we will ensure security . . . Jews and Arabs will coexist in Judea and Samaria as they do in Jerusalem, Ramle, Jaffa and Haifa."[16]

Begin has insisted that the five-year autonomy period outlined in the Camp David documents is merely to make arrangements for Arab inhabitants of the West Bank and Gaza to choose between Israeli and Jordanian citizenship. Those who become Israeli, he stated, would be entitled to the rights and duties of other Israelis; those who become Jordanian, would be given a special status as resident aliens. Since Jerusalem is an integral part of Israel, confirmed by Knesset laws passed in 1967 and 1980, none of the Camp David arrangements for autonomy apply to its residents, according to Likud. There can be no discussion about or compromise over Jewish settlements.

Begin and his heirs in Herut have stated that resolving the status of the territories does not require annexing the West Bank and Gaza for the simple reason that they are already part of Israel. The West Bank, Begin stated, "was liberated during the 6-day war when we used our right of national self-defense, and so it should be. . . . You annex foreign land. You don't annex your own country." Consequently, Judea and Samaria "are integral parts of our sovereignty. It's our land. It was occupied by Abdullah against international law, against our inherent right."[17]

Labor's Criticism of Autonomy

The Labor opposition was highly critical of Begin's version of autonomy. Former Foreign Minister and Labor Party leader Abba Eban argued that the Begin proposal to remove the boundary between Israel and any territory west of the Jordan River (the West Bank) was irreconcilable with Zionist objectives, which were "establishment of a Jewish state with a permanently assured Jewish majority and a sufficient measure of world recognition to enable the new state to function within the international system." Without separation of the predominantly Arab West Bank from the Jewish state, it would become necessary to impose Israel's authority on a disproportionate number of non-Jews, he stated. "Partition (of Palestine) reduced the imposition of Israeli rule on an Arab population to the degree compatible with Israel's security and a viable territorial expanse." The "sharp duality" of national identities created by history west of the Jordan River makes establishment of any unitary governmental structure in the area "artificial, coercive and morally fragile."[18]

"If you deny the existence of a boundary west of the Jordan," Eban argued, "you . . . expose Israel to inundation by an unassimilable Arab people that holds no national memory, vision, experience or dream in common with those of the state of Israel."

"Any attempt to reconcile the idea of a 'united Land of Israel' with the Camp David agreements reduces Israeli diplomacy to incoherence. To proclaim that 'there will never be a boundary west of the Jordan' is to say that Israel may one day become the only nation governing a foreign people permanently against its will and consent," the ex-Foreign Minister observed.[19]

A six-man committee of the Labor Party worked out a compromise recommending autonomy as a temporary measure, with future negotiations leading to a permanent arrangement with Jordan based on territorial compromise. It would ensure that Israel would have defensible borders through the establishment of "security zones" in the Jordan Rift, the Etzion Bloc of Jewish settlements near Hebron, and the southern Gaza Strip. Full Israeli "control" but not "sovereignty," would be maintained in these zones. Beyond the security zones, a single Jordanian-Palestinian entity would be negotiated over a period of time to be determined. Labor Party Chairman and former Chief-of-Staff, Haim Bar Lev stated that "autonomy with some areas under our full control is a lesser evil than autonomy over the whole of the West Bank."[20]

Notes

1. See *Census of Population and Housing (1967) East Jerusalem*, Central Bureau of Statistics, Jerusalem 1968, pp. xi–xii. An Israeli government census of September 27, 1967 enumerated 65,857 persons in "East Jerusalem." Of these 36 percent lived within the Old City walls. The city boundaries were extended by nearly 67 square kilometers as a result of the June 1967 war. The entire population of the extended Jerusalem municipality (104 sq. km.) was 265,000, 25 percent in East Jerusalem. The 1967 census compared to the 1961 Jordanian census showed a decline of 12.2 percent in the population of East Jerusalem.

2. See Yoram Peri, *Between Battles and Ballots Israeli Military in Politics*, Cambridge, U.K., 1983, pp. 58–59.

3. *Jerusalem Post Weekly* (JPW), no. 470, October 27, 1969.

4. See Yigal Allon, "Israel: The Case for Defensible Borders," *Foreign Affairs*, October 1976, vol. 55, no. 1.

5. See Don Peretz, "The War Election and Israel's Eighth Knesset," *Middle East Journal*, spring 1974, vol. 28, no. 2.

6. JPW, no. 669, August 21, 1973.

7. *New Outlook*, December 1973, vol. 16, no. 9 (146), January 1974, vol. 17, no.1 (147), pp.44–45.

8. Ibid., pp.71–72.

9. See David Schnall, *Radical Dissent in Contemporary Israeli Politics: Cracks in the Wall,* New York, 1979, chapter 9, "Gush Emunim: Messianism and Dissent."

10. See Appendix I, Begin's autonomy/peace plan of December 1977.

11. See Appendix II, Sadat's West Bank and Gaza proposals of July 1978.

12. By 1985 the West Bank Data Base Project headed by former Jerusalem Deputy Mayor, Meron Benvenisti, placed the number of West Bank Jewish settlers outside Jerusalem at 42,500 living in 114 Jewish settlements, a number considerably higher than the 28,000 to 30,000 usually estimated.

13. Tzvi Schuldiner, "Settlements: The Real Price Tag," *Haaretz,* July 25, 1980; articles by Elazar Levin on the subsidization and construction of West Bank settlements in *Haaretz,* December 17, 19, 21, 22, 23, 24, 1980.

14. For a systematic and relatively current discussion of changing Israeli settlement strategies and expenditures in the West Bank see, Meron Benvenisti, *The West Bank Data Project: A Survey of Israel's Policies,* Washington, D.C. 1984.

15. See Appendix I.

16. JP, April 30, 1979.

17. *Issues and Answers,* May 22, 1977.

18. JP, June 8, 1979.

19. Ibid.

20. JP, February 22, 1979.

5

Jewish Settlement in the West Bank

When Begin became Prime Minister in June 1977 there were 4,200 settlers in 36 West Bank settlements. By the beginning of the second Begin government in June 1981, the number had increased to over 30,000 settlers in over 100 settlements. Most were located in the hill country of the West Bank's northern and southern bulges. It is difficult to give a precise number of present settlements because of expansion through "thickening" and the spawning of subsidiary settlements like Maale Adumim A, B, C, and D. A reasonable estimate is that there are between 115 and 130 settlements inhabited by over 40,000 settlers in some 9,000 families (55 percent of whom are under 18 years old; the majority of the rest, between 20 and 40). Based on housing units already completed and under construction, estimates are that there could be an additional 40 to 60 settlements and a total of between 80,000 and 100,000 settlers by the end of the 1980's. Since the economic crisis of 1984-85 and formation of the new National Unity government the pace of settlement has lagged because of shortages in funding and the lack of enthusiasm for settlement by the Labor members of the government.

At present up to 70 percent of the land in the West Bank could be available for exclusive Jewish use under a variety of administrative and legal instruments used by the Israeli authorities. These devices include outright expropriation, closure for security or military purposes, classification of land as protected natural areas, confiscation for public purposes, and outright purchase. Acquisition and preparation of land for settlements, including planning, design, construction and installation of infrastructural facilities, and recruitment and absorption of settlers, are tasks performed by a complex array of officials, quasi-officials, and private organizations. Responsibilities frequently overlap, missions and practices change. At times these activities are closely coordinated, at other times there is vigorous competition for control of various dimensions of the settlement process. The diverse Jewish groups involved in settlement can be divided roughly into four categories: government agencies, the "National Institutions" (affiliated with the World Zionist Organization), ideologically motivated settlement organizations, and private commercial firms.[1]

The Bureaucratic Process: Government Agencies

In theory, the cabinet level Interministerial Committee on Settlement oversees and approves activities related to settlement in all occupied territory. Ariel Sharon served as chairman of this committee from his appointment as Minister of Agriculture in 1977 until he became Minister of Defense. He was then replaced by another militant nationalist, Yuval Neeman, leader of the Tehiya party. With formation of the new Government in 1984, the Interministerial Committee became inactive. The ministries most actively involved in settlement are Agriculture, Housing and Construction, Commerce and Industry, and Defense. In the Jordan Valley, where settlements were established on the basis of farming, the Agriculture Ministry was most important. However, because the Agriculture Ministry shares control of the Israel Lands Administration with the Jewish National Fund (the World Zionist Organization's land acquisition subsidiary), the ministry plays an important role in identification, seizure, and development of agricultural and nonagricultural land for settlement. During Sharon's tenure the ministry's role was enhanced to maximize land seizure and settlement.

While active in the Defense and Agricultural Ministries, Sharon was known as the godfather of the West Bank settlements. Following his shift to Minister without Portfolio, after his resignation from the Defense Ministry, Sharon was apparently forced out of decisions related to the settlement process. By 1983 the Agricultural Ministry's deputy chief, Mikael Dekel, became an active and influential member of the Interministerial Committee as Chairman of the Subcommittee on New Settlement. He advocated the offer of large incentives and heavy subsidies to the private sector as the best way to achieve a rapid increase of West Bank Jewish population. With the settlement of 100,000 Jews, in Dekel's view, it would be impossible for any future Israeli government to relinquish the West Bank.

Another, more recent, supporter of settlements is David Levi, Deputy Prime Minister and Minister of Housing and Construction in the second Likud government, who was a leading candidate to succeed Begin as prime minister. His views may be more pragmatic than ideological. Rumors that West Bank settlement was not among his top priorities undermined his candidacy among Herut Party veterans who elected Yitzhak Shamir as party leader and prime minister after Begin resigned in 1984. Despite the highly publicized steps of Levi's ministry to speed construction of housing projects, and the development of "build your own home" schemes, he was stung by criticism that he was responsible for long delays in expanding five large West Bank towns for which his ministry had prime responsibility–Maale Adumim, Maale Ephrayim, Ariel, Qiryat Arba and Efrat.

Under Levi's leadership, his ministry, in cooperation with other agencies, divided the West Bank into zones according to their distance from Israel's metropolitan areas. Land in these zones was received from the Israel Lands Administration by the Housing Ministry and delivered to public contracting companies, political groups, religious organizations, and other associations interested in settlement. Subsidies ranged up to 95 percent of land value and 40 percent of construction cost, depending primarily on the zone in which the land was located. The more distant from Israel's metropolitan area, the higher the subsidy.

Other ministries prominently involved in the settlement process have included Labor and Social Welfare, Science and Technology, and the Society for the Protection of Nature (part of Agriculture). Acrimonious disputes among those involved in the settlement process have occurred because of political competitiveness, and differences of philosophy and ministerial jurisdiction. Science Minister, Yuval Neeman, a militantly annexationist Tehiya leader, made it clear that the role of his ministry in the cabinet was to intensify West Bank and Gaza settlement. Neeman, one of Israel's leading physicists, pushed for locating high technology, computer-based and computer-related industries in the northern bulge of the West Bank, to make it a key part of Israel's economy and to generate employment for highly skilled Israeli workers rather than to create unskilled and semiskilled jobs for Arabs.

The most important government agency in the settlement process is the Military Government. The various ministries often work in the West Bank through the subdivisions of the military administration to expedite settlement and de facto annexation. For example, the Agriculture Ministry's control over the Israel Lands Administration has given it access to land and to land records. Land Administration officials are seconded to the Office of the Custodian of Absentee Property, a subunit of the Military Government. The responsibilities of this office include the discovery, demarcation, acquisition, and transfer of legally vulnerable tracts of land to various settlement institutions and organizations. During Ezer Weizman's tenure as Defense Minister, the cooperation of the Military Government was grudging and hesitant. Under Sharon and ex-Chief-of-Staff Eitan, the Military Government played an active role in the wholesale transfer of West Bank land from Arab to Israeli control. Military orders closing areas for security purposes were used to reserve land for current and future settlement. Military tribunals enforced strict interpretations of the documentation required to establish private land ownership as a means to circumvent the Supreme Court's ruling against expropriation of private lands for settlement rather than for security purposes.[2] Paramilitary Nahal settlements and smaller outposts or strong-points were widely used to establish settlements for "security purposes" and then later transformed into civilian settlements. Formation of "Yeshivot hesder" (field seminaries) permitted large numbers of Orthodox Jews to combine religious studies with West Bank army duty. Eitan issued orders in 1980 organizing West Bank settlers into local defense units, enabling them to fulfill their reserve army commitments by guarding and patrolling the vicinity of their settlements, an important aid to Gush Emunim settlement efforts.

Nongovernment Agencies

The Jewish Agency's Land Settlement Department, created after 1967 to carry out activities for which tax exempt funds contributed in the U.S. could not be used, is responsible for coordinating establishment of settlements under 300 families. Larger settlements are the responsibility of the Housing and Construction Ministry. Its two co-directors after 1967 differed radically on the Department's activities. Raanan Weitz, with a Labor background, bitterly opposed settlement, whereas Mattitiyah Drobles, with Likud affiliations, ardently supported Gush Emunim and advocated settlement of 1.5 million Jews in the West Bank within 25 years. Since 1977 Drobles had primary responsibility for the Department's activities beyond the green line while Weitz was left to complain about the lack of funding for settlement in the Galilee and the Negev, two underpopulated areas within pre-1967 Israel.

Tasks of the Jewish Agency's Land Settlement Department include advising the Interministerial Committee on Settlement about optimum locations, preparing long-range settlement plans, assigning approved sites to settlement movements and groups, facilitating settler absorption and helping with problems of social and economic adjustment, and serving as a legally convenient organization for land acquisition and allocation. During 1982, the Land Settlement Department completed a "Master Plan for the Settlement of Judea and Samaria and for the Development of the Area, 1983-1986," in coordination with the Agriculture Ministry and leaders of Gush Emunim. Approved by the government in 1983, the plan called for expenditures of $610 million in rural settlement programs beyond the green line by 1987; it included settlement of 50,000 more Jews in the West Bank by 1984, both in existing settlements and in 28 new ones, however that goal was not achieved because of Israel's financial crisis.

The Jewish National Fund (JNF) works closely with the Land Settlement Department in site preparation, paving roads to settlements, and in establishing infrastructure, through "Hemnuta," a company wholly owned by the JNF. Registered in Ramallah in the name of several of its directors, the JNF has been active in land purchases from West Bank inhabitants and from absentee land owners.

Numerous partisan-political and ideologically motivated organizations have also participated in and influenced Jewish settlement and de facto annexation. Until 1977, the most important organizations were various federations of collectives (kibbutzim) and cooperatives (moshavim). Although still active in settlement they have been overshadowed by newer established groups. The Labor-affiliated federations were prominent in settlement of the Jordan Valley, but after 1977, Gush Emunim emerged as the strongest group.

The Association of Jewish Local Councils in Judea, Samaria, and Gaza *(Yesha)* has become increasingly important. It publishes *Nekuda,* a biweekly journal, the recognized organ for discussion of issues important to settlers and Gush supporters. *Yesha* activists, all associated with Gush Emunim, led the unsuccessful "Movement to Stop the Retreat from Sinai," and are a forceful and effective pressure group/watchdog over government ministries and activities in the West Bank. *Yesha* and six West Bank regional councils created by the Interior Ministry to organize Jewish settlements, represent settler and Gush Emunim views; those affiliated with the Jordan Valley regional council are more Labor oriented.

These regional councils have received increasing powers from the Interior Ministry and the Military Government regarding zoning regulations, and judicial and tax matters related to the Jewish settlers. Although the entire West Bank has been divided by these six jurisdictions, the affairs of Arab inhabitants and control of areas outside the borders of their settlements do not fall within their administrative purview. Gush Emunim settlers, however, perceive the councils as the administrative and legal skeleton for the gradual extension of Israeli law and administration throughout the West Bank. Residents of West Bank Jewish settlements are not subject to either Jordanian or Military Government law, but are in a kind of extra-territorial status, under the jurisdiction of the Israeli legal system. Thus a dual control has been established, a Military Government for the Arab inhabitants and the laws of Israel applicable to Jewish settlers.

The Israeli Private Sector

Contractors, real estate agents, architects, construction companies, businesses and merchants are another important component in the extension of Israeli control on the West Bank. Their influence has grown since December 1982 when subsidization of private initiative began on a large scale. Real estate agents and land speculators have been active in detecting areas available for purchase. These middlemen assist in price negotiations, title transfer arrangements, gathering signatures from abutting land owners testifying to the authenticity of the seller's title and paying them "signature money." Land acquired in this way is then sold at a profit to the Israel Lands Administration which makes tracts available, in coordination with other agencies discussed above, to the Ministry of Housing and Construction. Real estate firms may also purchase land and engage private construction companies to build entire settlements. Alternatively, enterprises holding large parcels of land may sell plots to individuals who may then receive subsidized loans to build private homes. The terms of loans, grants and subsidies offered to new West Bank settlers were so generous that they attracted many middle class Israelis who once opposed the government's settlement schemes.

Loans with low or no interest were available for between $23,000 and $41,000 for construction of detached "villas," although the same type of government assistance was unavailable within Israel. Land was provided to construction companies by the Housing Ministry at only five percent of cost. Thus a full-size townhouse in Ariel, southwest of Nablus, cost less than an average apartment just across the green line, within Israel.

Similar subsidies were also available for Jewish businesses located in the West Bank on terms more advantageous than those in various Israeli "development zones." Moreover, such investments, unlike private housing investments, were insured by the government against the possibility of a future decision to evacuate the area. By 1983 dozens of Israeli businesses had taken advantage of these offers to initiate branches in the West Bank industrial zones.[3] Israel's economic crisis and emergence of the Labor dominated National Unity Government after September 1984 substantially diminished the scale and attractiveness of the subsidy programs available to Jewish settlers in the West Bank.

Tax advantages available to companies registering as Jordanian firms that operated in the West Bank included exemption from payment of national insurance contributions for Arab workers; exemption from real estate taxes (averaging $2,000 on a detached "villa" within Israel); exemption from certain service taxes and the compulsory "Peace for Galilee" 1982-84 war loan. Despite a court decision that Israelis working in the West Bank are liable to the same income tax as workers in Israel, it is legally impossible for income tax authorities to collect such levies because the West Bank is still technically part of a "foreign country" (Jordan). Additional opportunities and loopholes are available in foreign currency markets outside of Israel where the relatively hard Jordanian Dinar is legal tender. Income tax officials find it impossible to close all the loopholes exploited by tax evaders and speculators unless the West Bank becomes subject to the taxes and currency regulations in force within Israel. As a device to force full government jurisdiction over the West Bank, Jewish settlers at Kiryat Arba (near Hebron) sued to prevent imposition of taxes, in the hope that their action would hasten extension of Israeli law to the occupied territory. Government attempts to cope with these anomalies have led to the persistent, although gradual, ad hoc extension of Israeli jurisdiction into the West Bank by slight emendations of tax laws and military government regulations. This contributed to creeping administrative, financial and judicial absorption of the region.[4]

Government Water and Land Policies

The Israeli government's water and land policies in the West Bank are crucial in making these two relatively scarce commodities available for Jewish settlement and in restricting their use by the indigenous Arab inhabitants. In general, Israeli per capita consumption of water for domestic and agricultural use is about three times that of the West Bank Arab population. Israeli West Bank settlements with between two and three percent of the population were using about twenty percent of total water consumed in the area. About 96 percent of this was for agriculture. Control of West Bank water resources has been instituted by the Israeli government, and there has been discussion of integrating supplies on both sides of the green line. Israel's water commissioner acknowledged that a third of the water reaching Israel originated on the West Bank. The argument for integration is that Israel and the West Bank share a common aquifer system. Rain on the central mountain region seeps through to rock formations and drains either westward— toward the Israeli coast—or eastward—to the valleys from Mount Gilboa, the Jordan Valley and Dead Sea areas.

Although there is scanty evidence that some water resources in the West Bank are not being used, there are verified instances in which use by new Israeli settlements caused levels in Arab wells to dry up or become lower. A regional master plan for water supply is being prepared, indicating a change in emphasis from use by individual settlements to an integrated system.

Figures on Jewish land acquisition in the West Bank vary from 27 to 64 percent of the total 5.8 million dunams. Since 1979 most restraints or restrictions on land acquisition by Israel have been removed, enabling the government to seize almost any area required for settlement. Taking advantage of the Ottoman land code (see Part I) the Israel government has seized for Jewish settlement large amounts of *mawat* (dead) land on the outskirts of Arab villages. Another device was to seize land in heavily populated Arab areas for security or military purposes. These efforts were briefly thwarted by an unprecedented Supreme Court decision in 1979 banning establishment of a civilian settlement (Elon Moreh) on land acquired for military purposes. Since the Elon Moreh decision, the government has refrained from using expropriation "for security reasons" to acquire private registered areas. However, expropriation for access roads to settlements and major arterial highways has continued.

Because some two thirds of West Bank lands were never "settled" under the land settlement laws, i.e., rights to them having been secured by cadastral survey and entry in the official Land Registry, they are subject to definition as *mawat* and thus state property under the old Ottoman law. The Military Government has suspended all further "land settlement" procedures, i.e., the legal procedures for "settling" or determining ownership have been halted. Proving ownership of land that was not "settled" or marked by cadastral survey, has always been difficult and involved hearsay, word of mouth, and other types of evidence not usually accepted in Western courts of law. Furthermore, ambiguity in land ownership, caused by changes in the last years of Ottoman rule, is still a factor in many areas of the West Bank. Through strict application of Ottoman law Israel was able to "disestablish" ownership in many areas where Ottoman procedures for determining ownership prevailed for generations.[5] According to Benvenisti, "it is clear that by 1982 there are no more limitations of land availability in the West Bank for Jewish settlements. The exact amount of land is irrelevant. New Jewish towns are intensively being built . . . and a relatively small area can accommodate tens of thousands of settlers."[6]

Aware of the political importance of land-use planning and licensing, the Military Government amended the existing Jordanian Town and Village Planning Law of 1966. Arab planning and licensing authority was restricted to Arab municipalities; independent planning power of village councils was abolished; and planning power of district commissions was turned over to the Higher Planning Council of Israeli officials. Consequently, involvement of West Bank Arabs in land-use planning is now restricted to local Arab municipalities. Even licenses issued by local Arab commissions can be canceled by the Military Government which is authorized to halt or prohibit construction.

Until 1977 Military Government control of land-use planning was limited to specific areas such as military installations, roads and settlement areas approved by the Labor government (generally within the perimeters of the Allon Plan). "There was little effort to restrict Arab building and curb Arab spatial sprawl outside the built-up areas. As a result, extensive residential Arab housing developed, especially in the Jerusalem metropolitan area, and along arterial roads ('ribbon development')."[7] Since the Likud administration authorized establishment of Jewish regional councils, they have become "special planning commissions" with powers identical to those of Arab municipalities. In 1979 a new policy was adopted limiting Arab development by restricting land use to existing built-up areas and imposing severe land restrictions on all Arab-owned land outside nuclear towns and villages. The effect of this policy was to make open space outside existing built-up areas available for Jewish use, by checking future expansion of Arab towns and villages. This open space outside the limited areas demarcated for Arab use, "was defined as either 'special areas' (i.e., areas already seized or planned to be declared state lands for Jewish settlements), or as agricultural lands, nature reserves or areas for future planning."[8] "Knowing that Arab housing tends to follow new arterial roads in a 'ribbon development' pattern, the planners fixed extremely wide building lines on either side of the main roads, i.e. 100 and 150mm, to prevent Arab urban development along the roads to dissect existing Arab areas."[9]

Future Plans

General principles in planning new Jewish settlements include locating them with easy and swift access to the greater Tel-Aviv and Jerusalem regions, establishing road networks that make inter-settlement communication easy, and circumventing areas of Arab population. Plans for new settlements are supposed to be developed in consultation with a "Regional Council" in each planning sector, and if necessary should be referred to the Jewish "District Commission." Several larger urban settlements such as Maale Adumim, Kiryat Arba, and Ariel have their own planning commissions separate from the Regional Councils. Each settlement is a self-contained unit, but at the same time part of a regional or district plan in which a variety of services are provided.

During the Labor era the settlement concept focused on "pioneer" type outposts such as kibbutzim and moshavim. New settlements were thus oriented toward agriculture, necessitating arable land. Under Likud the emphasis has shifted toward urban settlement, which can be constructed on uncultivable or waste (*mawat*) lands. The new settlements are bedroom communities for Israeli urban centers, especially for Tel-

Aviv and Jerusalem. Most new settlement is urban, with plans for some 100,000 persons. Benvenisti believes that: "This figure is very high because of the absence of large numbers of ideologically motivated settlers who would go to 60 odd settlements situated in far, isolated areas. The main thrust of the prevailing settlement policies are the urban centers."[10]

As these plans for Jewish settlement proceed, the system of dual government, one for the Arab population and one for the Jewish settlers, has organized separate services in the following areas: posts, telecommunications, industry, taxes, agricultural marketing, school busing, vehicle licensing; and partially separate services in the supply of water, electricity, and roads. Obviously, the cost of establishing two systems with parallel but separate services is high. In 1982 the development and regular government budgets allocated for Jewish settlement in the West Bank were estimated at $150 million, about a third for housing, the rest for agriculture. Total West Bank investment by the government and the Jewish Agency by the end of 1983 was about $1.5 billion (excluding military investments), according to Benvenisti. Of this amount, $700 million was for housing and $75 million for roads—at $300,000 per kilometre. Another $2.5 billion would be required to reach the target of 100,000 Jewish West Bank settlers by 1986 (about $375 million a year, or more than double the rate of government investment in 1982). If the target date were to be 1991, the annual investment required would drop to $200 million. While these amounts are only a small percentage of the total budget, approximately $25 billion in 1981-82, they constitute a large proportion of the total allocated for development and other non-fixed items.

Israel's military and urban planners have divided the areas of Jewish settlement in the West Bank into four principal zones: The Jordan Valley, the Samaria and Judea mountain range, the extended urban hinterland around Jerusalem, and the greater Tel-Aviv urban hinterland. The zones are characterized as high, intermediate and low demand. In 1982 Benvenisti estimates that 66 of the over 100 Jewish settlements and towns already established will be of no demographic consequence. In most of the new settlements half the completed apartments are vacant.[11]

The Jordan Valley and Samaria-Judea mountain range are, and will remain, low demand areas with less than 25 percent of the Jewish settlers. In the Jordan Valley, Jews will constitute only 13.6 percent of the total regional population by 1991, and a mere 4 percent in the hill region. A maximum of 23,000 Jews in the hill areas, including those in towns like Kiryat Arba, are the projected figures, according to government planners cited by Benvenisti.[12]

The highest demand was and will probably remain for West Bank settlement areas that are within fifteen to twenty minutes commuting time from Tel-Aviv and Jerusalem. An exodus of people from central Tel-Aviv to West Bank suburbs had begun by 1982, and Benvenisti estimated that there was a potential for 50,000 to 60,000 more who would be willing to settle in the new dormitory housing projects then being constructed in western Samaria. The masterplan for Greater Jerusalem envisaged the boundaries of the capital stretching from Beit El in the north to Efrat in the south. Within this region 55.7 percent of the population was Jewish by 1983 and 44.3 percent Arab, with a slight increase for Arabs predicted by 1991. Within the greater Tel-Aviv area, between Kfar Saba in the north and Ariel in the east, Arabs made up 33 percent of the population and would comprise 35 percent by 1991.[13]

Within the two large urban high demand areas the populations are intertwined. It will be difficult to isolate separate areas with distinct Arab and Jewish majorities. Benvenisti predicts that economic and class distinctions between Jews and Arabs living within the same tightly inhabited urban regions would intensify inter-ethnic tensions. There is danger that the tensions will be even greater in the central sector because of the "fanatic nature" of a tiny minority of Jewish settlers who are attempting to establish control over the resources available to half a million highly politicized Palestinians.[14]

There is less danger of tension in the Jordan Valley where the combined Jewish and Arab population of 40,000 is not so intermixed. Jewish settlements in the Valley are located mostly in areas already seized for military purposes.

Repercussions Within Israel of Jewish West Bank Settlement

Only a small minority of Israeli Jews oppose any Jewish settlement on the West Bank. Even the Peace Now movement has called for suspension of further settlements rather than the removal of existing ones. Most critics of Likud policies toward the West Bank after 1977 focused on the types of settlement, the regions where they were located and other specific settlement, or military government policies. Results of public opinion polls fluctuate, so that it would be inaccurate to judge prevailing sentiment on the basis of any single survey. A poll published in the *Jerusalem Post* during November 1983 showed the inconsistencies of public opinion. Just over half of all Israelis polled were prepared to give up *all* or *some* of the West Bank in return for peace with Jordan. But the largest single group, 43 percent, opposed ceding any territory, even for peace. Only 9.3 percent were willing to cede all the West Bank, except Jerusalem, but 41 percent were willing to consider compromise in some areas. Only 3 percent were willing to give all territory including Jerusalem, 54 percent favored a freeze on new settlements, 22 percent were willing to dismantle some, and 31 percent refused to consider a freeze on new settlements.[15]

Sammy Smooha, an Israeli sociologist, has devised a rough summary measure or index classifying ideological positions on Israeli-Arab relations, taking into account attitudes toward West Bank policies such as annexation, Jewish settlement, territorial concessions, withdrawal of Israel to the 1967 borders with certain modifications, and coexistence of a Palestinian state in the West Bank and Gaza alongside Israel.[16]

Smooha distinguished six distinct ideological categories, identified by appropriate party designations: (1) Tehiya (since 1984 would also include Morasha), a party that was formed by dissenters from the Likud movement, members of Gush Emunim and the Greater Israel movement, calls for formal annexation and massive Jewish settlement in all the territories. It refers to Arabs on both sides of the green line as the "Arab minority," offering a choice between citizenship, resident status, or government-sponsored emigration, a euphemism for expulsion; (2) Likud, with the Herut party as its core, advocates the concept of Greater Israel with Jewish sovereignty over the West Bank and Gaza Strip. Likud has stopped short of calling for legal annexation, has pushed Begin's autonomy plan, but is internally divided on these issues; (3) Maarakh (until 1984 Labor Alignment—Labor party plus Mapam) advocates settlement for defensive purposes only in restricted, preferably uninhabited areas of the West Bank. Many of its leaders are prepared to make territorial concessions in the West Bank to permit a Jordanian-Palestinian confederation, and many of them supported discussion of the Reagan plan; (4) Dovish Jewish leaders including Mapam and Citizens Rights Movement, small, left-oriented Zionist parties supporting a Palestinian state alongside Israel in the West Bank and Gaza, some, even under PLO rule—if the PLO accepts certain conditions; (5) Rakah, the Israel Communist party and the new Progressive List for Peace, advocated total withdrawal from the occupied territories, including Jerusalem and establishment of a Palestinian state in the West Bank and Gaza; (6) Progressive National Movement, a small radical nationalist movement whose membership is predominantly made up of Arab students, does not recognize Jews as a nation or Israel's right to exist. It calls for establishment of a democratic-secular state in all of mandatory Palestine to replace Israel.

Smooha maintains that the prevailing consensus in Israel is defined by Likud and the Alignment despite the differences between them on borders and settlements. Although outside and to the left of Israel's operative consensus, the positions of Mapam, CRM and Rakah derive special significance because of their similarity to what may be called the "world's operative consensus." Despite its marginality in the Israeli context, the Progressive National Movement is significant because its positions correspond with those of several Arab states (Iraq, Algeria, South Yemen, and Libya).

The ideological distribution of the Jewish community in a survey conducted by Smooha showed that 88 percent of the public and 86 percent of the leaders fell into the Likud and Maarakh (Labor) positions. Within the Israeli mainstream, the less moderate (Likud) was outnumbered two to one by the more moderate (Maarakh). Jewish hawkishness varied significantly from one issue to another so that the percentage of Jews who were consistently hawkish could not be high. For example, Smooha demonstrated that 63 percent of all Jews classified favored existing frontiers including the West Bank and Gaza, but no more than 39 percent of all classified Jews supported settlements in Judea and Samaria.[17]

Few issues have divided Israelis so deeply and so bitterly as those related to the West Bank and its future, although they are divided more by differences of degree than principle. Only in the first of the five elections held since Israel occupied the West Bank was there extensive debate on the status and future of the territories. By the 1984 election for Israel's 11th Knesset, the West Bank question was relatively low on the agenda of the two major parties. Far more important were economic issues and Israel's occupation of Lebanon. One reason for the lack of discussion was division within the Labor Alignment. Preservation of party unity depended on preventing the emergence of political situations requiring decisive stands on the West Bank issue. Some observers believe that it was failure of Israel's leading parties effectively to express the intensity and variety of viewpoints on the issue that contributed to emergence of powerful extra-party movements such as Gush Emunim and Peace Now.

The Likud government's intensified repression of Arab dissidence on the West Bank during 1982, and the traumatic events and losses of the Lebanese War (portrayed by Chief-of-Staff Eitan and other government leaders as a struggle for Judea and Samaria), stimulated renewed debate on the future of the West Bank. In a Knesset session during October 1982, following hostilities of the Lebanese War, Prime Minister Begin depicted the choice facing the country as one between "the integrity of the Land of Israel or its redivision." The idea of territorial compromise associated with creation of a Jordanian-Palestinian federation was dismissed as equivalent to establishment of a PLO state. Begin reminded the Knesset that the issue of territory had long divided the Zionist movement between those who insisted on establishing and maintaining Jewish sovereignty over all Eretz Israel and those willing, for political or other reasons, to accept partition. The outcome of this debate, Begin argued, would determine whether Israel would live in security, in all the "land of our forefathers" or whether by removing "Judea, Samaria, and the Gaza district" from Israel's control, a PLO state would be established. Even if such a state were to emerge, he predicted that Israel's army would preserve its existence, but at the cost of still another war.[18]

Labor opposition leader Shimon Peres also perceived the problem as a profound choice between two fundamentally different paths. One, the "truly realistic path," involved "negotiations with Jordan—negotiations which will free the Palestinians from our rule and which are likely to ensure Israel's security needs." The other path was that of a "false and rhetorical Zionism" which will lead to Israel's end as a "Jewish state with moral values . . . into a country sunk in a dispute without end."[19]

The fundamental difference between the two arguments was Begin's emphasis on the historical rights of the Jewish people in contrast to Peres's emphasis on demographic problems, moral and social issues. Begin dismissed demographic issues as "false realism." The solution he offered was to organize relations between Jews and Arabs in a way that would prevent the Arabs from infringing upon Jewish rule of the country.

Peres advocated a peace settlement involving demilitarized zones, a united Jerusalem, and a series of interim agreements with Jordan based on substantial Israeli withdrawals from the West Bank and Gaza. Security rather than ideology would be the criterion for evaluating the terms of future agreements. Begin's vision of peace, on the other hand, resembled more a prolonged cease-fire imposed by Israel on an Arab world committed to Israel's dismemberment. Since Arab hostility was as intense as ever, he asserted, territorial compromise would only endanger Israel's security. The present status quo guaranteed security, with no Arab nation daring to challenge it. Why, then, he asked, invite "the enemy into our homes to undermine or prevent peace? . . . If the conditions created by our policy persist, we will live in peace and our sword will remain in its sheath."[20]

Subsidiary themes in the debate over the West Bank involve Israel's international isolation, its changing relationship with the United States, the future of relations with Egypt, the economic burden of defense and settlement programs, and the required policies to maintain order in the territories.

Basic principles of Alignment peace plans were reemphasized in the 1981 and 1984 election platforms. Accommodation with Jordan over the future of the West Bank became the central focus, with emphasis on replacement of the June 4, 1967 frontiers by "defensible borders." "The Israeli government will insist that, in time of peace, the security deployment of the IDF forces and of settlements in certain areas, including: the Jordan Valley with the northwestern shore of the Dead Sea, Gush Etzion, the environs of Jerusalem, and the southern Gaza Strip will be included within the sovereign territory of Israel."[21]

"The Jordan River is Israel's eastern security border. No foreign army will cross the western bank of the Jordan. The territories to be evacuated by the IDF west of the Jordan will be demilitarized; in addition to such demilitarization, Israel will insist on vital security arrangements."

Jewish settlement in these specified zones "is vital for the security of the state." Although a Labor government would not establish new Jewish settlements in densely populated West Bank Arab areas, "no [existing] Jewish settlement will be uprooted, and the settlements will be allowed to remain in place."

Labor's 1984 platform criticized Likud's West Bank policies and administration, asserting that Begin's "domination of Judea, Samaria and Gaza has already undermined the democratic and moral foundations of Israeli society." The Alignment rejected Likud's policy of "not one inch" as subversive of peace and liable to transform Israel "from a state with a clear Jewish majority into a bi-national state, contradicting the Zionist and democratic nature of the state of Israel and weakening it internally."

The Alignment stated willingness to "transfer broad powers and responsibilities on civilian matters to the local authorities and to civilian elements" in the occupied areas. While maintaining "complete authority," the Alignment promised to respect the "rights of the citizens" and to show concern for their well-being. Labor would "insist on the protection of individual rights, the maintenance of law and order, and the equality of all residents before the law." To establish permanent Israeli rule over the Arab inhabitants of the territories, stated the platform, was inconsistent with "maintenance of a democratic society guarantying equal rights for all its citizens." Labor denounced the emergence of a Jewish underground terrorist group that sought retaliation against Arabs in the territories for their attacks on Jewish settlers, and promised to "firmly and decisively . . . uproot every instance of the[ir] violation of the law. These phenomena which run counter to all Jewish and human ethics grew out of the annexationist policy [of Likud], a mystical nationalistic ideology, and the rejection of any compromise solution."

Labor agreed with Likud not to recognize the PLO "and any other organizations based on the Palestinian Covenant which denies the State of Israel's right to exist." Nor would Labor agree to "establishment of another Palestinian state in the territory between Israel and Jordan [east of the river]." Rather, the Alignment insisted that the Palestinian problem be resolved "within a Jordanian-Palestinian framework. The Jordanian-Palestinian state will include the territory of Jordan, most of whose residents are Palestinians, and well-defined, densely populated areas in Judea, Samaria and Gaza which will be evacuated by the IDF forces with the establishment of peace," provided of course, that the evacuated areas remained demilitarized and subject to Israeli security control. These arrangements would be negotiated by representatives of Jordan and "authorized representatives of the Palestinian Arab residents of Judea, Samaria and the Gaza Strip . . . and [other] Palestinian individuals, . . . who recognize Israel and reject terrorism."

Labor failed to gain sufficient votes to form its own coalition in the July 1984 election. Instead a National Unity Government (NUG) was created with Likud as an equal partner and seven other parties as members. Although Labor party leader Shimon Peres became prime minister, his deputy and minister for foreign affairs was the Likud leader, former prime minister Yitzhak Shamir. Peres thus had to water down the Alignment's election peace plans.

The agreement which served as the basis for the NUG promised the Arab residents of the West Bank and Gaza a voice in determining their own future. Jordan would be invited to enter the peace negotiations but in the event of internal disagreement within the Israeli government over territorial concessions, new elections would be held. The NUG agreement emphasized Likud and Labor opposition to establishment of a Palestinian state "between Israel and the Jordan River," and to negotiations with the PLO. However, large-scale implementation of Likud's goals was thwarted by the stipulation that "During the period of the unity government, no sovereignty, Israel or other, will be applied to Judea, Samaria and the Gaza District." New Jewish settlements would have to be agreed on by the members of the NUG (rather than the score or more which Likud had promised, Labor agreed to establish only five or six).[22]

But the greatest constraint on full implementation of Likud's settlement policies and on rapid integration of the West Bank into Israel after 1984 was the severe financial crisis facing the country. The new NUG found itself unable to continue the financial largesse previously available for expansion of the Jewish presence in the area. Within the cabinet there were debates over allocating even a small percent of the more than $300 million annually that Likud had earmarked for its West Bank projects.

Economic and demographic arguments against annexation or continued Israeli occupation of the administered territories were strongly reenforced in a study published during 1984 by the International Center for Peace in the Middle East. The study, written by Dr. Simha Bahiri, a senior researcher at the Middle East Economic Cooperation Project of the Interdisciplinary Center for Technological Analysis and Forecasting, Tel-Aviv University, is titled, *Peaceful Separation or Enforced Unity: Economic Consequences for Israel and the West Bank/Gaza Area.* The author assumes that "one cannot have peace with the territories. Even the de facto non-belligerence which some would argue we have now implies large defense budgets and lost exports."[23]

If Israel were to give up the West Bank and Gaza, states Dr. Bahiri, its GNP, projecting from present trends, would reach $40 billion by 1995, or 7.5 billion more than if the occupation were to continue. Per capita income would reach $7,690 rather than $6,500 if the territories were exchanged for peace. GNP less defense costs would be 45 percent higher after a decade of peace in contrast to present projections based on continued hostilities. West Bank and Gaza GNP would also increase, to $4.3 billion instead of $2.5 billion if the territories were separated from Israel and attached to Jordan in some form.

Continued Israeli occupation will raise the cost of defense to nearly $8.5 billion by 1995, or 26 percent of GNP. Without the territories, defense costs would drop to only $5.2 billion or 13 percent of GNP. Continued occupation would increase defense costs at a greater rate than the annual GNP growth rate, according to the study.

Israel's demography will be greatly altered with continued occupation, states Dr. Bahiri. Without separation, the Arab population will reach nearly 40 percent of "greater" Israel by mid-1990s, but would be only 22 percent within the 1967 borders. Even the Jewish population of Israel would increase at a more rapid rate without the territories, to 4.3 million instead of 4 million by 1995.

But what if Israel should resolve its economic problems and a Labor led government were to take office? The Labor party has indicated that it would go ahead with an "improved Allon plan" which includes the south Dead Sea area and half of the Hebron region. This would incorporate a broadened Jordan Valley and an expanded Kiryat Arba to include all new Jewish settlements in the Hebron region. During a visit to the Jordan Valley early in 1985 Peres expressed agreement with the resolutions of the United Kibbutz Movement (Labor) calling for annexation of these regions. Other staunch advocates of the "improved Allon plan" include Labor's Minister of Absorption, the Minister and deputy Minister of Agriculture, and the Defense Minister.[24]

After formation of the NUG, U.S. Secretary of State George Shultz urged Peres to initiate measures to "improve the quality of life" for West Bank Arab inhabitants. Indications of policy modification were agreement by Peres to diminish restrictions on activities of outside investors and American organizations working in the West Bank; appointment by the Ministry of Defense of hand picked Arab officials to replace Israeli army officers who had taken over posts of many local Arabs discharged by the previous Likud government because of their nationalist activities or sentiments; and a lower keyed rhetoric in policy pronouncements about the future of the area. Still, under Defense Minister Yitzhak Rabin, any overt manifestations of sympathy for the PLO or for an independent Palestinian state by the area's Arab inhabitants continued to be outlawed.

Some Israelis are concerned that debate over the West Bank, associated with other political issues of the day, may polarize the country into violent factionalization. One aspect of the rift is that it frequently corresponds with class and ethnic differences. In the hawk-dove spectrum, doves tend, proportionately, though not uniformly, to be Ashkenazi, middle or upper class, well-educated, and nonreligious. Those favoring a hard line toward the Arabs and permanent control of the West Bank and Gaza tend to be Oriental, lower class, lacking education, and more religious.

The dividing line in polls on the question of the West Bank is between those unwilling to relinquish any part of the West Bank and those willing to trade parts of it for peace; only a small minority is willing to give up the whole area. Several intellectuals have warned that this volatile mixture of ethnic, class and political differences could lead to civil war. While some spokesmen for the Herut party believed that the threat of civil war was exaggerated, several of them agreed with an editorial in Israel's largest mass circulation newspaper, *Yediot Achronot,* that it was time to place limits on freedom of speech and assembly to reduce possibilities of violent clashes in the polarized and overheated political arena.[25]

The most sensitive and potentially explosive phase in evolution of the West Bank problem in Israeli politics is likely to occur just before annexationists and anti-annexationists perceive that a "point of no return" will be passed; when Arabs sense that it will be too late to negotiate acceptable territorial compromise with Israel given the implantation of Jewish settlements, infrastructural ties between Israel and the territories, and Israel's ideological commitments; and there is growing perception of inability or unwillingness by the United States to place meaningful pressure on Israel to move toward compromise.

Many Israeli journalists covering the West Bank as well as some scholars including Benvenisti are convinced that de facto annexation has proceeded so far that no Israeli government can now reverse the process. In fact, some Israeli doves, frustrated in their efforts to thwart annexation, have despaired of further anti-annexationist activity and have shifted from a struggle against annexation to a struggle for equal rights for Arabs in the territories, assuming that they will be integrated within Israel's borders.

Benvenisti believes that even a Labor-led coalition would lead only to a change in style rather than a change in substance of policy for the West Bank. Extreme religious and historical claims would probably be avoided, but "in fact, a Labor victory would probably set off a new wave of settlers who would insist on going to the West Bank for ideological reasons."[26] A freeze on settlements and territorial compromise "would be unlikely to produce practical results." The most recent "moderate" Labor formula for territorial compromise proposes to annex 40 percent of the territories along with nearly 40 percent of their inhabitants. Previous Labor governments made much more attractive offers to King Hussein which he rejected.

Domestic political constraints also argue against changes in a Labor government's West Bank policy. The only potential coalition partners for a Labor-led government are some combination of religious parties, with the NRP as its core. While it may be remotely conceivable that the NRP could be persuaded to "suspend" further settlement, it is nearly impossible that it would agree to reverse the process of integration that has occurred since 1977 under Likud. Furthermore, unlike the Jewish settlements which were abandoned in Sinai, those in the West Bank are much closer to "home," integrated into the country's electricity, water, and other service networks, and are deeply imbedded in the emotional and patriotic consciousness of large numbers of Israelis. The divisiveness in Labor has infected it with a paralyzing ineffectiveness in dealing with the diverse questions of the West Bank, or in forming a coherent and consistent policy. Despite the clarity and logic of arguments presented by many leaders within the Alignment like Abba Eban and Peres, against absorption of the territories, their approach is nullified by the complex of forces which perceives that Israel's destiny is its territorial "wholeness."[27]

Notes

1. Much material in this chapter comes from a working paper prepared by Ian Lustick; for a detailed discussion of administrative devices and legal instruments used by the government of Israel to secure West Bank lands for Jewish settlement see Meron Benvenisti, *The West Bank Data Project A Survey of Israel's Policies,* Washington, D.C. 1984, chapter 4, "The Scramble for Space: Land Ownership." Summary of study in *The New York Times,* April 1, 1985, pp. 1, 6.

2. For a close analysis of the administrative and legal mechanisms used to achieve transfer of West Bank lands from Arab to Jewish control, see Ian Lustick, "Israel and the West Bank after Elon Moreh: The Mechanics of De Facto Annexation," *Middle East Journal,* Autumn 1981, vol. 35, no. 4, pp. 557–577.

3. See articles published by Elazar Levin in *Haaretz,* during December 1982.

4. See Shlomo Maoz, "Judea and Samaria as a Tax Shelter," *Haaretz,* April 15, 1983.

5. Concerning the use of Ottoman land law and the interrupted Jordanian "deed settlement" process for the expropriation of West Bank land see Lustick, "Israel and the West Bank after Elon Moreh . . ." 1981, op. cit.

6. Meron Benvenisti, *The West Bank and Gaza Data Base Project Study Report,* mimeographed 1982, p. 35.

7. Ibid., p.36.

8. Ibid., p.38.

9. Ibid.

10. Ibid., p.62.

11. See article by David Richardson, "Settlements and Suburbia," which discusses Benvenisti's analysis in JPW, no. 1,197, October 9–15, 1983, p. 13.

12. Ibid.

13. Ibid.

14. Ibid.

15. JPW, no. 1,203, November 20–26, 1983.

16. See Sammy Smooha and Don Peretz, "The Arabs in Israel," *Journal of Conflict Resolution,* September 1982, vol. 26, no. 1, pp. 451–484.

17. Ibid.

18. The Knesset speeches of Begin and Peres referred to were delivered on October 18, 1982, and transcribed in full in the *Daily Report for the Middle East and Africa,* Foreign Broadcast Information Service, October 19, 1982, pp. 11–114.

19. Ibid.

20. Ibid.

21. *New Outlook,* June/July 1984, pp. 24–25. Same source for following paragraphs.

22. JP, September 12, 1984, "National Unity Government Agreement (Abridged)."

23. JPW, No. 1, 250, week ending October 28, 1948, p. 17.

24. Prof. Ze'ev Sternhell, *Al Ha-Mishmar,* March 29, 1985.

25. *Yediot Achronot,* February 18, 1983.

26. See article by Meron Benvenisti, "The Turning Point in Israel," *The New York Review of Books,* October 13, 1983, pp. 11–16.

27. For a discussion of the degree of flexibility Israel may still have toward the future of its relationship to the West Bank see Ian Lustick, "The West Bank and Gaza Issue in Israeli Politics," in Steven Heydemann (ed.), *The Begin Era,* Boulder, 1984, pp. 79–98, and Ian Lustick, "The West Bank: How Late is Too Late?" *Moment Magazine,* March 1985, vol. 10, no.3, pp. 16–19, 58–60.

6
The Military Government Administration

Labor's Military Government

The ambiguity and indecisiveness of Labor toward the West Bank was often reflected within the defense establishment. Dayan and his entourage, who represented the Rafi faction of the Labor party, claimed that the territories were under military occupation and should be administered by the Defense Minister. Veteran leaders of the mainstream old Mapai, including the Prime Minister and Finance Minister Sapir, tried to keep management of the territories out of the Defense Ministry to prevent their Rafi[1] competitors from enhancing their political power. A key question was whether representatives of other ministries in the territories—health, agriculture, education, etc.—should be subordinate to the Minister of Defense, to their home ministries, or to the cabinet.[2]

Initially a Military Governor was subordinate to the Chief-of-Staff and Minister of Defense. He was assisted by a General Staff of functionaries, appointed by the various ministries and answerable to them. The cabinet also established a Ministerial Committee on the Occupied Territories, headed by Sapir, with the intent of overseeing Dayan. Prime Minister Eshkol reserved certain powers for himself, such as political negotiations with inhabitants of the territories.

Decisions on the territories were taken at three levels: the cabinet, the ministries, and the regional and district military commands. The Cabinet Committee, headed by the Prime Minister, established major policy; the Inter-Ministerial Committee for the Coordination of Activities in the Territories handled security and political problems; economic affairs were the charge of the Director-General's Committee for Economic Affairs; the Unit for Coordination of Activities in the Territories, in the Ministry of Defense, coordinated all nonmilitary operations. In the West Bank the Military Governor had full legislative and executive authority. As Military Governor there were few restrictions on his powers: his authority has been compared to that of a head of state. In the struggle between the defense establishment and the rest of the government, the IDF seemed to win the upper hand, and Dayan became popularly known as "the King of the Territories."

The most important official in the Military Government network was the coordinator, a major-general who headed the Military Government Division of the General Staff and was the Chief-of-Staff's principal adviser on issues related to the territories. Unlike many of the Military Governors at regional levels who were often reservists, the coordinator was a professional officer.

The legal device by which the Military Governor of the West Bank became its virtual chief-of-state was proclamation number 2, issued by the military commander on June 7, 1967. It was specific and categorical, stating in part:

> All powers of government, legislation, appointment and administration in relation to the Area or its inhabitants shall henceforth be vested in me alone and shall be exercised by me or whoever shall be appointed by me to that end or acting on my behalf (Article 3(a)).

In effect, this proclamation transferred the powers of the former Jordanian government, previously exercised by the District Commissioner (Mutasarrif), to the Israeli military commander. Municipal and judicial powers remained, in theory, in the hands of former local officials.

Initially the military government structure went through several changes. Eventually, the office of Coordinator of Activities in the Administered Areas was established, lasting until 1981 when it was replaced in the West Bank by a new "civil administration." The coordinator supervised relations between the various functional ministries operating in the West Bank.

Legal Issues

From the beginning of the occupation the Israeli government perceived itself as a permanent, sovereign power, rather than as a de facto occupying power under international law. As the "lawful belligerent occupant" of the West Bank, Israel agreed to comply only with the "humanitarian" provisions of the Hague 1907 and Geneva 1949 Conventions. Although the legal status of Jordan's 1950 annexation of the West Bank was disputed, Israel's provisional acceptance of the conventions obviated an automatic transfer of sovereignty to the State of Israel. The ambiguity of this position was underscored by decisions of Israel's Supreme Court which examined Military Government legislation in the context of the international conventions, ruling that the legislative power of the military was limited to changes required to maintain law and order, to requirements dictated by military necessity, and to serve the well-being of the civilian population.

Since 1967 there has been a constant tension between the courts and the military with regard to occupation policies in the West Bank. Contrary to the Conventions, all Israeli governments since 1967 have adopted policies and enacted measures changing the status quo. The court ruled in 1980, however, that any legal or administrative change should be "intrinsically temporary, and its principal function is to do the utmost to maintain public order and security . . . the existing law requires that the regional commander refrains from initiating changes in the region unless there are special reasons for doing so." The court interpreted "special reasons" for changing existing laws as those contributing to the well-being of the local residents.[3] However, the more than 1,000 military orders that have been issued since 1967 have had the cumulative effect of new legislation, negating both the Conventions and the principles enunciated by the Supreme Court. As Benvenisti has observed, these military orders provide a record of legislation that many a parliament might envy. One reason for this is the simple procedure required to make laws. "The Military Government possesses unlimited power, there are almost no checks and balances. Only a very small number of orders reach the bench of the High Court of Justice. The political input of the Minister of Defense, the only person accountable to the Knesset, is negligible, and the knowledge of Knesset members about the legislative activities affecting the lives of almost 1.3 million people, is nil."[4]

Although Military Government ordinances are called "security legislation" most of them deal with economic, administrative and judicial affairs. Usually, rather than enact new laws, amendments are introduced to existing Jordanian legislation or the Military government issues orders that borrow from Israeli laws.

At the beginning of the occupation, Defense Minister Dayan stated that the Military Government would operate on the principle of "non-intervention," i.e., military officials would limit their involvement in local affairs. The intent was to limit areas of friction between the local population and Israelis. Thus, by the mid-1970s only 650 out of some 16,000 West Bank officials were Israelis.[5] Nevertheless, Israelis continued to control the most influential positions.

In accord with the Labor Government's policy of "non-intervention" municipal elections were held in the West Bank during 1972 and 1976. Both were conducted, technically, according to Jordanian law, although the law was amended in 1976 to permit women's suffrage. (A third municipal election scheduled for 1980, during the Likud administration, was not held because of West Bank unrest.) Israeli policy also kept in place much of the Jordanian administrative and judicial structure, although all government offices and departments were supervised by Military Government officers and Israeli officials seconded to the Military Government from various civil ministries.

It soon became evident to Dayan that the "non-intervention" policy was incompatible with the establishment of "new facts" intended to integrate much of the West Bank infrastructure, such as the road system, water supply, electricity grid, and trade and commerce, with Israel. To begin with, such integration required intervention in many aspects of life among West Bank inhabitants, from the ways in which they earned their livelihood in agriculture, to obtaining permits for trade, commerce, travel, and a host of other activities. Furthermore, many of the inhabitants refused to accept Israeli jurisdiction over the West Bank. Protests by the inhabitants against Israeli policies resulted in ever increasing intervention by the Military Government and other security agencies in everyday activities. To prevent the spread of nationalist sentiment, many school textbooks were censored or banned; the Arabic press was also monitored and censored; several hundred individuals suspected of activities conflicting with Israeli policy were imprisoned without trial or expelled from the West Bank; homes of those suspected of nationalist activities by the Israeli security authorities were often destroyed; curfews were imposed; and in many areas during much of the ten years of Military Government under the Labor administration, a full regime of martial law existed.

Dayan initially attempted to deal with the local population through its established elite structure, in much the same way as the Jordanian, British and Ottoman rulers who preceded him. On the one hand, an attempt was made to coopt mayors, mukhtars, and other local officials by extending travel privileges and personal courtesy visits, and even vaguely promising to establish a Palestinian autonomous entity of some type (never explained in detail). A major innovation was Dayan's "Open Bridges" policy, intended to ease the strains of Arab daily life under military occupation. Shortly after Israel's occupation began, the bridges across the Jordan River were repaired and opened for two-way traffic between East and West Banks. With authorization from the Israeli military government, West Bank Arab residents were permitted to travel to Jordan and beyond, and Arabs from abroad who received Israeli permits were allowed to visit the West Bank and Israel. Not only personal visits, but trade and commerce was initiated, expanding to a large scale in which the exchange between the two banks eventually became a major part of the economy in each. Dayan believed that the "Open Bridges" policy would hasten the normalization of life in the occupied

West Bank and diminish tensions which might have been exacerbated by family separations and economic dislocations. At first the policy was considered risky by many Israelis but the Military Government authorities who controlled the crossing procedures managed to contain, if not eliminate, any security risks.

On the other hand, the formation of any political groups was prohibited, and attempts by local leaders to establish a West Bank consultative association were forbidden. Any attempt to establish a region-wide political, social, or even cultural activity had to be strictly monitored by the Military Government, and was thus discouraged.[6]

Likud's Military Government Innovations

In November 1981, the Likud government authorized the military administration in the West Bank to proceed with a measure that would allegedly move toward unilateral implementation of autonomy for Arab residents. The measure, Military Order 947, established a "civilian" administration for the area to "look after the civilian affairs of the local inhabitants." The order separated military and security affairs from civilian matters. However, the "Head of the Civilian Administration," was appointed by the IDF area commander. He was an Israeli reserve colonel, Menachem Milson, a professor of Arabic language and literature at the Hebrew University, whose recommendations on how to deal with the PLO and militant Arab nationalism in the West Bank caught the attention of Defense Minister Sharon. The official Israeli position was that the civil administration would gradually be taken over by local Palestinians who would assume administrative tasks formerly undertaken by the Military Government. Milson interpreted civil administration to be, not "an administration operated by civilians but an administration dealing with the affairs of civilians."[7]

Order 947 was regarded by the Israeli government as the first phase in the implementation of the Camp David agreements providing for "withdrawal" of Israeli military and civilian administration from the West Bank. The order replaced the title, Military Commander of Judea and Samaria with the new title, "Commander of the Israeli forces in Judea and Samaria"; the West Bank now ceased to be a separate military government district, and became an "area" in which Israeli forces were stationed, in the same way in which they were stationed in various "areas" of Israel. Not only was a separate Military Government "abolished," in the West Bank, but in accord with the Camp David agreements, it was "withdrawn" and placed under the Central Command outside the West Bank. Despite the changes in titles, Military Government jurisdiction continued in the West Bank and the commander of Israeli forces in the "area" would continue to hold the powers under proclamation Number 2 of June 7, 1967.[8]

Milson, although he held only powers of subsidiary legislation and was subordinate to the chief of the Military Government, had all the powers transferred by the Military Government since 1967 from the Jordanian monarch and government to the Israeli Military Governor. This included matters removed by the military from the jurisdiction of local courts to Israeli military courts and tribunals. With these powers, Milson was able to implement his program of delegating limited authority to West Bank Palestinians who were willing to cooperate with him, such as the Village Leagues, organizations of West Bank rural notables formed with Israeli encouragement to resist pressure from pro-PLO nationalist factions.

The rationale of the Milson program was discussed in an article he published in the May 1981 issue of *Commentary* magazine, "How to Make Peace with the Palestinians." He argued that Israel's failure to "play by the rules" of Middle East Arab politics and Dayan's "non-intervention" policies had enabled the PLO to dominate politically the Arab population of the West Bank. Consequently, he asserted, the PLO had become firmly entrenched, as evidenced by its success in the 1976 local elections when PLO candidates won the mayoralities and local councils in more than a score of towns and villages. PLO success, Milson argued, had "silenced" the majority which was eager to negotiate with Israel, but had been prevented from voicing its opinions by threats from the PLO. As a result, West Bank politicians were reluctant to participate in the peace process and to engage in autonomy talks, leading to a deadlock in the tripartite Israel-Egyptian-U.S. peace negotiations. Dayan's proposal for unilateral transfer of civil authority to West Bank mayors was rejected by Milson as an open invitation for the PLO to take over and a *coup de grâce* to moderate Palestinians. He concluded that total departure from previous Israeli policy in the West Bank was essential to eradicate PLO influence and to encourage the moderates. Milson's program was to take advantage of traditional inter-Arab divisiveness as expressed in the West Bank by rural-urban tensions. The PLO, according to his perception, was backed by urban elites, such as those who won the local elections. To counteract their influence, a rural resurgence would be encouraged through support of the Village Leagues, whose members were regarded by the city residents as "illiterates," according to Mayor Freij of Bethlehem, antisocial elements known to be thieves or land brokers.

The "rules of the game," according to Milson, involved offers to those who cooperated with him of financial patronage, priority in employment and housing, establishment of a Regional Development Fund to disburse money to Village Leagues for construction, as well as extending League authority in regions where it was situated. While offering every "encouragement" to "cooperative" elements, pressures were intensified on those who were unwilling to "play the game." Millions of Saudi-supplied dollars provided to PLO supporters were cut off; personalities and institutions through which PLO influence was exercised were punished in various ways; harsher methods were used to "pacify" militant nationalists such as the students in the four West Bank universities and the publishers of PLO-inclined Arabic newspapers. Within a few months the mayors of the largest West Bank cities were dismissed, the pace of expulsions was increased, and curfews, demolition of houses, seizure of property, and imprisonment without trial were used with increased frequency.

Measures taken to implement Order 947 in November 1981 aroused strong protest, not only in the West Bank, but within Israel itself. By the end of 1981 it seemed that the West Bank was on the verge of full-scale civil insurrection. Many Palestinians, as well as Israelis, regarded the new West Bank "reforms" as a move toward annexation rather than an attempt to increase the civil authority of the inhabitants. The four universities, Bethlehem University, University of Hebron, An-Najah (Nablus) and Bir Zeit (near Ramallah), were the focal point of opposition and were closed by the military authorities for weeks or months at a time. Refusal by Municipal Councils to deal with the new "civil" authorities was met with the imposition of curfews, removal of municipal officials and their replacement by Israelis, usually army officers. Rioting against intensification of the army's counter measures spread through most of the towns of the West Bank and to Gaza. There were several bloody clashes between protesters and the armed forces with unrest greater than in any of the previous thirteen years of occupation. Against the advice of Milson, the army Chief-of-Staff, General Rafael Eitan, issued directives to increase personal and collective punishments and to give local Jewish settlers in the West Bank (mostly members of Gush Emunim) greater freedom to combat unrest.

Within Israel, IDF policies in suppressing the unrest and opposition to the new "civil" administration were attacked by editorials in most of the major newspapers; in the Knesset by the Labor opposition; and by scores of university professors and other professionals. The *Jerusalem Post* observed, in an editorial on March 22, 1982, that: "It is hard to believe that anybody in his right mind expects the army's punitive measures to cause the Palestinians to warm up to the idea of autonomy." *Haaretz,* the leading independent paper, compared Milson to an Indian reservation governor, accusing him of blowing up houses, arresting labor leaders, appropriating land and banning the distribution of hundreds of books.

Events in the West Bank and the policies of the Likud government were suddenly overshadowed during June 1982, and for the following year, by Israel's invasion of Lebanon. Indeed, many observers perceived the invasion as a move by the government to strengthen its position in the West Bank through elimination of the PLO in Lebanon, thereby destroying its influence among Arab nationalists.[9]

After formation of the NUG in September 1984, there was little change in the structure, management and operation of the Military Government. The "Civil Administration" initiated by Likud continued as part of the Ministry of Defense under a Coordinator of Activities in the Administered Territories. In accord with Prime Minister Shimon Peres' promise to U.S. Secretary of State George Shultz to "improve the quality of life" in the territories, a number of American and Arab investors were authorized to investigate possibilities for investing in the West Bank through the Business Group for Middle East Peace and Development formed in New York. Restrictions were removed on import of personal funds by the Arab inhabitants and loans and grants to West Bank municipalities and institutions received from Arab states were eased. Israeli military government officers reported by early 1985 that nine local West Bank authorities had been permitted to import $2.5 million in Jordan dinars during the previous nine months and that between $3 and $4 million in Jordan dinars had been made available to West Bank beduin by the Amman government. Plans were also authorized for opening an Arab bank in Nablus. The NUG also eased military government censorship of Arabic books and decreased the number banned from over 1,500 to some 300 by mid-1985.[10]

On the other hand, the NUG's Defense Minister, Yitzhak Rabin, made clear that strict political controls would be continued. Shortly after assuming his post, Rabin's Military Government officers summoned ten former members of the National Guidance Committee (banned by Sharon in 1982) to inform them that any attempt to revive the Committee would be punished. In February 1985 the opposition Citizens Rights Party (CRM) issued a report of alleged discrimination by the Israeli government against West Bank Arabs. As an example it noted that in Jewish settlements south of Bethlehem, there were 7,000 telephone lines, but only 260 permitted for the Arab population which was several times the size of the Jewish. It stated that the government persisted in its policies of blocking economic growth in the Administered Territories and had turned them into "auxiliaries of the Israeli economy"[11] (see Chapter 8, West Bank Economy).

Notes

1. Rafi, an offshoot of the once dominant Mapai labor party was formed by Ben Gurion and others who advocated a national or "statist" approach to Israel's problems rather than emphasizing labor's "rights." Members of Rafi tended to advocate more militantly nationalist foreign and defense policies than did other members of the Labor bloc. Rafi reunited with Mapai when the two factions joined Achdut Avoda to form the new Labor Party in 1968.

2. See Yoram Peri, *Between Battles and Ballots . . .* , op. cit. pp.90–93, passim.

3. Israel High Court of Justice decision 351, 1980.

4. Meron Benvenisti, *The West Bank and Gaza Data Base Project Pilot Study Report,* 1982, op.cit., pp.40–41.

5. Peri, op.cit., p. 92.

6. For an extensive favorable discussion of Labor's military government policies, see Shabtai Tevet, *The Cursed Blessing: The Story of Israel's Occupation of the West Bank,* London, 1970.

7. See Michael Oren, "A Horseshoe in the Glove Milson's Year in the West Bank," in *Middle East Review,* fall 1983, vol. xvi, no. 1, pp.17–29.

8. See Camp David Agreement, Appendix III.

9. *The New York Times* of May 28, 1985 reported that U.S. Ambassador to Israel, Samuel W. Lewis, disclosed in an interview with Israeli television that in a meeting with Defense Minister Sharon during December 1981, at which Sharon revealed Israeli plans to invade Lebanon, he (Sharon) observed that the invasion would help "solve the problems of the West Bank and Gaza."

10. JPW, no. 1, 281, week ending May 25, 1985, p.13; no. 1,265, week ending February 2, 1985, p. 8.

11. JPW, no. 1,268, week ending February 23, 1985, p. 9, no. 1,251, week ending October 27, 1984, p. 4.

7

The Arab Dimension

Demography[1]

Three months after it occupied the West Bank, Israel conducted a census showing an Arab population of nearly 600,000, a net loss of over 200,000 people since the last Jordanian estimate in 1967. The population was distributed in the areas shown in Table 1.

By 1974 the population increased to 661,600 at an average annual rate of 2.2 percent. By the end of 1982 the West Bank population, excluding Jerusalem, was 710,000, or 110,000 less than it had been on June 3, 1967, despite fifteen years of an estimated annual 3.5 percent natural increase. Table 2 gives estimates of West Bank population from June 1967 to 1982, showing fluctuations in population size with the gradual and slow replenishment of Palestinians living there.

The primary cause of West Bank population decline since 1967 has been emigration. The first mass exodus was during and immediately after the 1967 war (June to December) when some 234,300 Palestinian Arabs left, representing about 28.5 percent of the total population. That exodus accounts for 43 percent of the total population decline since 1967. The remaining 57 percent occurred between 1968 and 1982, averaging a loss of 8.5 percent a year. Between 1968 and 1975 the overall population increased at the same rate as before the 1967 war. After 1975, the rate of change decreased, again due to emigration, until the yearly increase declined to 0.6 percent in 1980.[2]

The rate of natural increase in the West Bank was influenced by a high birth rate (gross 44 per thousand compared to 35 per thousand of Israeli Arabs), a high death rate (15 per thousand) and high infant mortality (82 per thousand). Despite a natural population increase of 14,000 (1968) to 20,600 (1980) per year, the constant migration, totaling some 100,000 between 1969 and 1980, was equal to half the natural increase. In 1980, 83 percent of the natural increase of 20,000 was diminished by the emigration of 17,000 West Bank Arabs.

Between 1969 and 1974, when migration slackened, many West Bank Arabs were employed in Israel, commuting from their homes to work.

TABLE 1

Distribution of Population According to Districts, 1967 Israeli Census and
1961 Jordanian Census (Density per sq. km. urban, rural, and refugee settlements)

District	1967 Israel Census	1961 Jordan Census	Density per Sq. Km.	% Urban Settlements	% Rural Settlements	% in Refugee Camps
Hebron	118,358	117,768	112.1	32.4	62.6	5.0
Bethlehem	49,515	54,777	87.6	52.2	35.6	12.2
Jerusalem	29,904	31,302	105.3	(a)	81.9	18.1
Jericho	9,078	63,980	26.9	58.5	9.7	31.8
Ramallah	88,877	118,839	114.9	24.6	68.2	7.2
Nablus	152,381	170,452	96.0	27.4	61.3	11.3
Tulkarm	72,229	83,600	217.6	26.5	63.0	10.5
Jenin	78,295	79,193	137.0	10.7	82.9	6.4
Total	598,637	729,804	108.7			

(a) excludes East Jerusalem

Source: Israel Defense Forces, West Bank of the Jordan Gaza Strip and
Northern Sinai Golan Heights Census of Population 1967 conducted by the
Central Bureau of Statistics, Publication no. 1 of the Census of Popula-
tion 1967, Jerusalem, 1967. (compiled from tables on pp. 1X, X1, XIX)

The economic boom in Israel during this period drew heavily on low
paid labor from the occupied territories. During 1975, economic conditions in Israel began to deteriorate, marked by rapid inflation and
recession. Consequently work opportunities for Palestinian youth in
Israel were diminished, and many began to look abroad, especially in
the Gulf.

The population of the West Bank is very "young," with 45 percent
under the age of 15. However, the age structure is not stable, fluctuating
constantly since 1961.

Between 1967 and 1980 those in the 15-29 age group fluctuated
between 25 and 29 percent. A disproportionately large number of the
1967 emigrants came from the latter group, with only a small number
from the 0 to 14 group. Thus the remaining population was depleted
of 15 to 29 year olds. By 1980, the 0 to 14 group had moved into the
15 to 29 category accounting for its increased size. Furthermore, many
West Bank males were working abroad during the 1967 war and did
not return, also contributing to depletion of the 15 to 29 group. This
trend is marked by a substantial increase of females, to well above 50
percent in the 25 to 29 age group, reaching 59 to 60 percent in the 35
to 44 age group.

Immediate demographic implications of these figures are an increasing
proportion of fertile females, and an increasing proportion of youths
leaving school, entering the job market, and facing the choice of well-
paid employment abroad, or remaining in the West Bank under the
disadvantages of military government. Obviously, a high percentage of
youths have opted for employment abroad.

TABLE 2
Population in Eastern Palestine Between Pre-June 1967 and 1982 (estimated)

Date	West Bank	Jerusalem	Eastern Palestine Total
1967			
June 1	820,000	80,000	900,000
Sept. 1	599,377	66,000	665,377
Dec. 31	585,700	66,000	651,700
		(as of December 31)	
1968	581,700	69,000	650,700
1969	595,200	72,500	667,700
1970	603,900	76,134	680,000
1971	617,300	81,000	698,300
1972	629,000	86,300	715,300
1973	646,200	91,000	737,200
1974	661,600	95,000	756,600
1975	665,100	97,500	762,600
1976	670,900	99,500	770,400
1977	681,200	103,776	784,976
1978	690,400	108,000	798,400
1979	699,600	114,200	813,800
1980	704,000	118,400	822,400
1981	707,700	122,000	829,000
1982	710,000	125,000	835,000

Adapted from: Janet Abu Lughod, "Demographic Consequences of the Occupation," MERIP Reports, June 1983, p. 16.

The gross marriage rate (number of marriages divided by total population) was also greatly affected by the 1967 exodus. Most marriages occur in the 15 to 29 age group (constituting the largest number of those who left in 1967); thus the number of those eligible for marriage was greatly depleted, particularly males. As the 0 to 14 group subsequently reached marriageable age, however, there was a steep rise in the marriage rate, especially between 1968 and 1972. The decline in marriages between 1972 and 1976 might be attributed to economic conditions, although this is speculative.

The age specific fertility (ASF) (the annual number of births per thousand females in a particular age group) in the West Bank more than doubled among women under twenty, and increased in the 20 to 24 group. In all age groups above 25 there was a decrease of ASF. Two possibilities occur—larger number of females marrying at a younger age, but with a decrease in the frequency of conception. The most probable explanation for the decline after 25 is that contraception is becoming increasingly widespread in the West Bank, a hypothesis confirmed by West Bank gynecologists and clinics. Reasons given for earlier marriages are that with increased income, more men can afford to pay dowries earlier, and the possibility that the size of dowries has decreased.

Total fertility, i.e., the sum of ASFs, which gives an estimate of how many children an average woman will bear, shows a progressive decrease since 1967. This points to increased use of birth control. Although there has been an increase in the proportion of 15 to 29 year olds since 1967, and an increase in that group's fertility, there has not been an increase in the gross birth rate, pointing to the widespread use of contraception, and to the absence of husbands who are working abroad.

Cultural influences also may have contributed to the increased use of birth control. Large numbers of West Bankers are coming into contact with Israelis through their work and many are purchasing television sets. Television provides both alternative values to those of the traditional village, and it offers night-time entertainment which could contribute, as it has in many other environments, to a reduced birth rate.

Within the West Bank there have been decided regional variations in demography. During the 1967 exodus, there were three areas from with emigration was very high: The Jordan Valley which lost more than 50 percent of its inhabitants, perhaps because the East Bank was immediately accessible; frontier villages near Ramallah, many of which before 1967 had been subjected to Israeli retaliatory raids; and the border areas near Hebron where there was a history of conflict with Israel. Conversely, there was only a 20 percent rate of emigration from the northern hills around Nablus.

The lowest birth rates in 1968 were in Ramallah and Bethlehem, and by 1979, they had declined even further. Reasons given for their low birth rates are closeness to Jerusalem, which left them open to its cultural influences, and to economic benefits from work in and associations with the city. Temporary emigrants from these two Christian areas tend to work or study in Western Europe or America and are thus absent for longer periods than those who travel to Arab countries from where they return more frequently; Ramallah has a particularly high emigration rate which tends to deplete the more fertile population and thus lower the birth rate; the larger Christian population of these two towns is more culturally conditioned to birth control.

Since 1968 there has been a fairly high birth rate in the northern regions of Jenin, Tulkarm, and Nablus. Hebron, the most conservative region and the most predominantly agricultural, had a higher birth rate in 1968, and an even larger increase by 1978.

Between 1968 and 1970 there was a net migration from West Bank villages to towns (25.6 percent lived in towns during 1968, 29.1 percent in 1970) continuing the urbanization trend that began early in this century. Evidence suggests that the trend continues. The urban birth rate has traditionally been lower than in rural areas, and by 1972 the urban rate in the West Bank had declined.

Estimated Birth Rates for Urban and Rural Areas

	1968	1972
Urban	0.041	0.038
Rural	0.044	0.046

The Christian birth rate is lower than the Muslim, corresponding with Christian concentration in towns. In 1974 Christians were 5 percent of the West Bank population, with 61 percent living in towns. Their birth rate of 0.016 compared to the Muslim rate of 0.047.

The importance of Jerusalem in West Bank demography cannot be overlooked, demonstrating how inseparable the city is from the totality of the region. Benvenisti points out that: "The shift in West Bank population distribution is closely related to the concentration of Arab population in the Jerusalem metropolitan area."[3] Estimates indicate that 37 percent of the total population of the southern subdistricts lived in Arab Jerusalem in 1969, 50 percent by 1980. Almost all West Bank laborers working in Jerusalem during 1980 (13,900) came from the Ramallah, Bethlehem, Jericho and Hebron subdistrict; 90 percent of them commuted to work. A third of the total work force in these subdistricts was employed in Jerusalem. All Arabs from Bethlehem and Jericho, 50 percent from Hebron, and 60 percent from Ramallah, who work outside the West Bank, are employed in Jerusalem.[4]

Conclusions from these demographic observations are that emigration from the West Bank has been increasing since 1975. An observation based on the assumption that the proportion of 20 to 30 year-old population will continue to increase until about 1987 as the 1967 0 to 5 age group reaches maturity. With Jewish settlement of the West Bank expected to reach 100,000 before the end of the century, employment opportunities will be concentrated in low-paid, unskilled labor. Consequently, many Arabs in the 15 to 29 age category will leave to search for opportunities elsewhere. However, evidence suggests that such opportunities will greatly diminish in the Gulf and in neighboring Arab countries. Although the West Bank Arab birth rate is still high, the analysis of birth rates shows that notwithstanding an increase in the proportion of young females with high fertility rates, the gross birth rate of the West Bank has remained fairly constant. This strongly suggests a trend of increasing birth control. Thus, once the majority of 1967 0 to 5 year-olds are married it is probable that the gross birth rate of the West Bank will decline.

"Considered together, these two factors clearly predict that within the next five years the Arab population of the West Bank will begin to decrease."[5]

Political and Social Change, 1967–1973

> With the June War, all previous modes of life were shattered. The whole social structure was challenged. All previous values and convictions were put to the test. . . . Something basic was wrong. The organization of the society, the values, the ideals were all upset (Aziz Shehadeh, "The Palestinian Demand for Peace, Justice and an end to Bitterness—," *New Middle East* No. 35 August 1971:22).

Although exaggerated, these sentiments of Aziz Shehadeh, a Ramallah lawyer, reflect the sentiments of large numbers of West Bank Palestinian Arabs after 1967. In reality, several years passed before there was a discernible change in West Bank political and social leadership. In most areas the traditional social structure remained intact. Villages and rural areas continued to be dominated by towns and cities, where the influential families remained at the apex of society, under control of the Israeli military authorities. Land ownership and public stature acquired from professional, religious or political involvement were still the most significant factors in attaining influence. Families which had been influential for generations like the al-Masris and al-Tuqans of Nablus, al-Khatibs of Jerusalem and al-Ja'baris of Hebron remained powerful. These, the "notable" families, had been close to the monarchy in Jordan and had earlier supported annexation by the Hashemites. The extent of their influence was evident in the 1972 municipal elections when the traditional elites maintained much of their authority and position.

Initially many of the notables attempted to "strike a deal" with the Israeli occupying authorities. Two weeks after the 1967 war ended, thirty of them offered to cooperate with Israel in exchange for permission to establish a West Bank state. Not only was their offer rejected by the Military Government, but all further political meetings or consultations among the notables was banned. In addition, the occupation undercut many of the traditional activities and roles of the notables and municipal leaders. It soon became obvious that the Israeli military governors rather than the traditional elites were the real repositories of power by virtue of their control over travel, commerce, construction and nearly any other activity for which municipal permission was required.

At the local level, management of affairs was left with the existing municipal governments, and Jordanian municipal law remained in effect.

However, the long list of municipal prerogatives, e.g., zoning, planning, development, industrialization, public services, budgeting, etc., were subject to scrutiny and approval of the occupation authorities. Control of water supply, electricity, gas and sewage disposal was supervised by the military. Often, rather than city managers, mayors became the intermediaries between the local population and the military authorities.

Israeli military control of municipal affairs was underscored in the budgeting process. While the municipalities were authorized to generate revenues through levying taxes and raising grants from outside, most expenditures were controlled by the military government. Israeli grants and loans were supplemented by Jordanian government subventions, and by funds raised from other Arab sources. Following the 1976 elections, cities in other Arab countries established pairing relationships with a "sister city" in the West Bank. Thus, if the city of Ramallah received a million dollar gift from the city of Algiers, Israeli authorities required that the sum be deposited in a specific bank in Jordan; only small amounts could be brought to Ramallah at one time. When a need for the funds arose, Ramallah government officers had to receive approval from the occupation authorities. Often such approval was denied, forcing the local officials to turn to the military government for emergency funding. In times of political stress, the military often withheld approval for receipt of Arab funds, and also denied Israeli emergency funding. Disbursement of these funds, however, often gave local municipal officials an important role as the source of Arab largesse.

Initial political discontent seemed to be "managed" by a vaguely defined National Front or National Union which was held responsible for a wave of strikes, demonstrations and sabotage during 1967-1968. The Front was believed to be an offspring of Suleiman Nabulsi's National Socialist Party that had been in the vanguard of opposition to the Hashemite regime during the 1950s and was thus opposed to those loyal to Jordan. From 1968 until 1973, there were no overt Front activities or organizations.

The October War to 1977

By 1973 changing political configurations in the wider Arab world and growing impatience with the Israeli occupation began to have an impact on political and social developments in the West Bank. Despite economic assistance from Jordan, West Bank Palestinians began to turn against the King because of his repression of the PLO, especially during the 1970-1971 "civil war." On the international scene, the PLO was emerging as a significant political force and its leader, Yassir Arafat, was acquiring increasing international recognition. The October 1973 war was perceived as an Arab victory, the first over Israel by any Arab nation. All of these events provided a fertile ground for intensification of more militant Palestinian nationalism.

Within the West Bank and other occupied territories, Israeli policy emphasized strict control over all aspects of Arab life—health, refugees, local government, education, school textbooks; and the number of deportees for political reasons was increasing. The convergence of all these events and trends led to increasing nationalist sentiment among the Palestinians and growing disillusionment with the pro-Jordanian traditional elites.

Rise of PLO Influence

In January 1973 the Palestine National Council decided in secret to establish a National Front in both the West Bank and Gaza as the political base for a future Palestine state. The Palestine National Front was formally established in August 1973, as a coalition of independent politicians and groups including supporters of Fatah, the Democratic Front, the Communist Party, the Ba'ath, and the Popular Front. It declared itself "an inseparable part of the Palestinian national movement represented in the Palestine Liberation Organization."[6]

Jordanian reaction to appearance of the Front on the West Bank was a vigorous campaign to regain influence. Hundreds of Palestinian political prisoners were released or amnestied and a press war opened between pro- and anti-Hashemite Arab journals published in Jerusalem. Front activity became increasingly overt, directly challenging the Israeli authorities with protests against military government policies and calls for Palestinian self-determination. Attempts by the Israeli security authorities to crush the PNF with hundreds of arrests and detentions only inflamed nationalist sentiment, distanced relations between the pro-Hashemites and the West Bank public, and led to intensification of repressive measures.

In the period between 1973 and the second West Bank municipal elections in 1976, the PLO and the Israeli government appeared to be competing for influence over the Palestinian public. In the hope of winning hearts and minds, Defense Minister Shimon Peres introduced a "civil administration" plan in October 1975, including added authority for municipalities and placing Arab officials in charge of administrative offices. Eventually the municipalities and departments were to receive authority over all civil matters. But few Palestinians were attracted by the Peres scheme. Even the old elites, the notables who had won the 1972 election, and with whom the Israelis believed they had established rapport, rejected the proposals. Overwhelmingly, Arab sentiment among moderates and radicals insisted on an end to the occupation. Hikmat al-Masri, the Nablus prototype of the West Bank traditionalists, argued: "The very idea of 'autonomy' in the occupied territories is an insult to the dignity of the Palestinian people . . . and we refuse it with all our strength."[7]

Meanwhile the PLO was acquiring increasing credibility as the representative of all Palestinians, including those in the occupied territories. Its information offices, communications media, research and financial bureaus, welfare, educational, medical, police and diplomatic services began to take on the characteristics of a quasi-government. In the West Bank its agents gradually superseded those of Jordan and loyalties were shifted from the Hashemites to the Palestinian organization. One indication of this shift was the behavior of political deportees from the West Bank. Until 1973 most deportees, like the former Arab mayor of Jerusalem and the president of the Sharia Court of Appeals, found refuge in Amman. Several were even given cabinet posts. After 1973 most of the prominent deportees turned to the PLO and many were given important positions in that organization or in the Palestine National Council.

The best evidence of the shifting political trends was the outcome of the 1976 municipal elections. Unlike 1972, when the PLO and West Bank nationalists opposed participation, in 1976 the PLO decided that the National Front should seize the opportunity to gain control of the municipalities thereby depriving the pro-Jordanian merchants and notables and the hand-picked Israeli candidates of their influence. The Jerusalem daily, *Al-Sha'b,* argued that the nationalists should participate in the elections to undermine the "traditional" leaders. Hopeful of counteracting nationalist influence, the military government announced that the vote would be extended to women and propertyless men. The mayors of Tulkarm, Nablus and Ramallah, as well as several women's societies protested that Israel's change of the electoral regulations violated the Geneva Conventions on occupied territories and a few nationalist women refused to vote because the right had been provided by Israeli intervention.

The election campaign became heated, with nationalist blocs forming in many areas under the slogan: "No to [Peres'] civil administration, Yes to the [Palestine] National Front." Because the military authorities banned public rallies or the use of overtly nationalist slogans (many posters did flaunt the red, green, black and white colors of the Palestinian flag), campaigning took place in informal gatherings in homes and clubs.

Seventy-two percent of the 88,000 eligible voters (of whom 33,000 were women) participated in the election on April 12, 1976. The nationalists won overwhelmingly in Hebron and Beit Jala, and obtained strong majorities in Nablus, Ramallah, al-Bireh, Tulkarm, Beit Sahour, and Jericho. The greatest upset was in Hebron where the pro-Hashemite Jabaris were displaced by young professionals in the national bloc. Only in Bethlehem did the incumbent non-PNF mayor, Elias Freij, keep his post. But even he observed that the new mayors and council members represented a better educated, younger and more outspoken group of politicians. Several of the newly elected nationalists did not hesitate to express their overt support for the PLO. Bassam Shak'a of Nablus observed: "The elections proved clearly that the Palestinians believe their sole legal representative to be the PLO."[8]

Palestinian Politics Under Likud

During the remaining year of Labor government in Israel, efforts by Peres to undermine the influence of the Nationalist Front were unsuccessful. Nor were attempts by the Begin government between 1977 and 1981 to curb PLO influence any more fruitful. Fresh tactics were attempted after Menachem Milson was appointed to head the new civil administration in November 1981. The chief political device in the Milson program was to establish alternative political organizations to the Nationalist municipal councils, called Village Leagues.

The first Village League was established in 1978 at Dura in the Hebron area, by Mustafa Dudin. Between 1948 and 1968 Dudin had been an Egyptian appointed official in Gaza, then he moved to Jordan. There Dudin rose rapidly to become Minister of Social Welfare, Ambassador to Kuwait, and an appointed member of parliament. In 1975 he returned to the West Bank to reside in the Hebron area.

Overcoming initial Israeli discouragement, in 1978 Dudin formed an organization ostensibly for rural resurgence, dedicated to the development of villages which had stagnated while the cities flourished. He believed that the bread and butter issues of concern to the villagers had been neglected by the urban nationalist politicians. Dudin also advocated strong ties with Jordan and perceived its 60 percent Palestinian population as artificially separated by the East Bank-West Bank division. He was openly critical of the PLO National Covenant and called for direct negotiations with Israel as the only way to solve the Palestinian problem. Dudin's support for the Sadat peace initiative, Palestinian participation in the autonomy talks, and advocacy of the Reagan plan placed him in opposition to prevailing pro-PLO sentiment among municipal leaders and other opinion makers in the West Bank.

These views and Dudin's outspokenness caught the attention of Milson who sought to promote him and the Village Leagues as a "more legitimate" representative of the West Bank population, and as an alternative to the pro-PLO leadership. Indeed, when the new alliance between the Leagues and Milson became obvious, two leaders of the organization were assassinated. In Beirut, WAFA, the PLO news agency, proclaimed that the organization "had carried out a people's sentence against the two agents." At the other end of the spectrum, the Jordanian Prime Minister warned in March 1982, that any West Bank resident joining a Village League would be condemned to death. Subsequently nineteen members of the organization published statements disassociating themselves from the Leagues. At this point, Milson decided to arm Village League guards.

Milson's attempt to use the Leagues to legitimize his new Civil Administration, to undermine West Bank nationalist leadership, and to gain support for Begin's version of the autonomy plan, backfired. Attempts were also made to force villagers to recognize the Leagues by giving them authority to issue permits for travel, trade, and other necessary functions. Mukhtars were pressured to form new Leagues and villagers were "encouraged" to attend their rallies. League officials were given leeway in using force to deal with their opponents among the population. In one instance, a League rally held in Hebron was guarded by the Israeli army and border police. When Milson dismissed most of the elected West Bank mayors and disbanded municipal councils that refused to cooperate with him, he won the League's approval. Israeli efforts to establish communal order by discharging the elected pro-PLO leadership led to the rise of vigilantism by Jewish settlers and branches of the Village Leagues against nationalist demonstrations, and increased unrest throughout the West Bank.

In 1982 the six active Leagues formed the Federation of Palestinian Leagues, headed by Dudin, with headquarters in Ramallah, and in 1983 they proposed formation of a political party under Dudin to be called the Democratic Movement for Peace. However, the resignation of Milson in 1982, and the appointment of a new Defense Ministry Coordinator of West Bank Activities, Shlomo Iliya, cast a shadow of uncertainty over the future of the Leagues. The new Coordinator quickly disassociated himself from the Leagues and announced that he was interested in a dialogue with other West Bank leaders, such as the deposed mayors of Ramallah, Nablus and Halhul.

Growing hostility to the Leagues among their potential constituency led them to draft their own "Palestine National Covenant" in 1983.[9] Many of its provisions, and other new policies adopted by the six Leagues then active in the West Bank such as support for the Reagan plan, placed them on a collision course with the annexationist policies of the Likud government. In addition to supporting the Camp David agreements, the covenant also called for recognition of the "legitimate rights of the Palestinians" as well as the rights of the Israeli people "to live within recognized and legal borders." By 1984, with establishment of the NUG and a new Military Government administration, the Village Leagues all but disappeared from the political scene.

In the last few years, secular nationalism has had to compete with religious Islamic nationalism on the West Bank on a small scale. With the rise of Islamic fundamentalist movements in the surrounding countries, revivalist activity has also appeared on the West Bank. In late 1981, the Muslim Brotherhood won election to the student council in al-Najah University in Nablus and made an impressive showing in the student election at Bir Zeit University near Ramallah. The Jordanian branch of the Muslim Brotherhood, an offshoot of the Egyptian Brotherhood, is known to have a substantial following in the West Bank. Another offshoot of the Jordanian Brotherhood, Hizb al-Tahrir al-Islami, and the Harakat al-Tawhid (Unity [of God] Movement) also have West Bank supporters. In addition to contacts with the Jordanian organizations, they are strongly influenced by Islamic groups, based principally in Kuwait, Egypt, and Saudi Arabia. Brotherhood groups have maintained good relations with the Jordanian government which tolerates passive manifestations of Islamic militancy.

The general ideological orientation of the Islamic fundamentalists is opposed, not to the nationalist consensus, but to its secularist tendencies. They maintain that when a Palestinian state comes into being, it should be Islamic in nature, orientation and policy, and based on the tenets of the Koran. The Unity of God Movement opposes Arafat, King Hussein, and the Iraqi Ba'ath, but supports the Islamic Republic of Iran. These organizations reached their high point during 1982 when the Islamic revival was flourishing in surrounding Arab countries, but since then they seem to have lost their momentum.[10]

The Palestine Communist Party, a remnant of the pre-1967 Communist movement in the West Bank, still functions underground and its leaders were active in organizing the National Front. Because it was among the first groups to call for dialogue with Israeli leftists, it was an outcast in the nationalist mainstream until 1974. Since 1977, when the two-state solution to the Palestine problem became the centrist position, the PCP has again become "respectable" in nationalist circles. Its current position on the national question is identical to that of the Israeli Communist movement, Rakah. The two groups signed a joint communique in Moscow during December 1982, calling for mutual recognition between Israel and a Palestinian state; they also endorsed the Soviet Middle East peace plan and the Arab peace resolutions adopted at the Fez summit in 1982.[11]

The pro-Jordanian trend (other than the Village Leagues) has been steadily losing influence since the late 1970s. It still represents the older, traditional politicians and former Jordanian officials, including individuals such as Mahmud Abu Zuluf, editor of the Jerusalem *al-Quds* newspaper, Hikmat al-Masri, former Mayor of Nablus, Anwar al-Khatib former Governor of Jerusalem, Anwar Nuseibeh of Jerusalem, a former Jordanian Cabinet member, Rashad al-Shawwa former Mayor of Gaza, and Elias Freij, a mayor of Bethlehem, the only West Bank Arab mayor not removed in the mass discharge of "nationalist" officials during the Milson era. This group of "King's men" still perceives unification with Jordan as the most likely viable solution to the political problem of the Palestinians. Their specific positions include support for the Fez plan, legitimacy of the PLO, recognition of UN resolutions 242 and 338, guarded backing for the "positive elements" in the Reagan plan, mutual recognition of Israel and the Palestinians, a Jordanian-Palestinian confederation, and a call for the PLO to delegate King Hussein the authority to negotiate on its behalf.[12]

Disappointment swept this group following collapse of the Arafat-Hussein discussions in 1983, and many of them blamed Arafat and the PLO for the breakdown. They felt that the PLO was not truly aware of the "facts on the ground" created by the occupation and by the debilitating effect which it has had on the inhabitants. Hikmat al-Masri observed that: "About half the land in the West Bank has already been taken by the occupation, while the PLO still argues over the differences between a state and a confederation!"[13]

As a result of the growing tensions between PLO leader Yassir Arafat and the Syrian government, Arafat sought to rebuild his ties with Jordan during 1984 and 1985. Dissent within the PLO and in Arafat's own Fatah organization led to internecine fighting among the diverse Palestinian factions in Lebanon and divisions between factions aligned with Syria and those remaining loyal to Arafat. Syria threatened a showdown with Arafat supporters when they held a meeting of the seventeenth session of the Palestine National Council (PNC) in Amman during November 1984. Although boycotted by the pro-Syrian factions, the PNC meeting represented a majority of Palestinian nationalists and it strengthened their links with King Hussein leading to a formal accord in February 1985 signed by the King and Arafat. The accord called for:

1. Total Israeli withdrawal from the territories occupied in 1967 and a comprehensive peace settlement.

2. The right of self-determination for the Palestine people within the context of a proposed confederation of Jordan and Palestine.

3. Resolution of the Palestine refugee problem in accord with U.N. resolutions.

4. Resolution of the Palestine question in all its aspects.

5. An International Conference representing the five permanent members of the U.N. Security Council and all parties to the conflict including the PLO as part of a joint Jordanian-Palestinian delegation, to conduct peace negotiations.

The significance of these events on the West Bank was that they diminished the competition and political differences between Arafat supporters (comprising the majority of political activists) and the "king's men," those who perceived a solution in a West Bank-Jordan federation. Indeed, by the middle of 1985, King Hussein took the initiative in fostering such an approach to peace in parleys he held in Washington with President Reagan and other American officials. The major stumbling block to progress remained U.S. reluctance and Israeli refusal to negotiate with official representatives of the PLO despite support for the organization and for Arafat as its leader by the great majority of West Bank Palestinians.[14]

A poll of West Bank public opinion on national issues conducted in June 1983 by the magazine *Al-Bayader Assiyasi,* revealed the following trends:

(This poll was conducted in the last week of June 1983. A random selection was taken from all sectors of a total of 777 citizens. Special forms were distributed for this purpose and included seven important questions. These are the most important results.)

Question 1: Do you agree to the continuation of Yassir Arafat as leader of the Palestinian march?

Yes: 716 (92.15%)
No: 42 (5.41%)
No opinion: 19 (2.44%)

Question 2: Do you support the continuation of the Jordanian-Palestinian dialogue?

Yes: 559 (71.95%)
No: 183 (23.55%)
No opinion: 35 (4.5%)

Question 3: Do you support initiating an Egyptian-Palestinian dialogue?

Yes: 431 (55.47%)
No: 293 (37.71%)
No opinion: 53 (6.82%)

Question 4: Do you think that the United States will exercise practical pressures on Israel?

Yes: 213 (27.42%)
No: 535 (68.85%)
No opinion: 29 (3.73%)

Question 5: Do you think that Syria will withdraw its forces from Lebanon within an American framework?

Yes: 582 (74.9%)
No: 131 (16.86%)
No opinion: 64 (8.24%)

Question 6: Do you support the Arab peace project of the Fez Summit?

Yes: 585 (75.29%)
No: 128 (16.47%)
No opinion: 64 (8.24%)

Question 7: Do you support the continuation of the Palestinian contacts with the Israeli peace forces?

Yes: 443 (57.04%)
No: 248 (31.9%)
No opinion: 86 (11.06%)

Social and Cultural Affairs Under the Occupation[15]

Press

During the first few years of occupation, the West Bank Arabic language press, mostly located in Jerusalem, was permitted relatively free political expression. Although censorship began to increase gradually after 1969 on "security grounds," the Arabic press was openly critical of many Israeli policies and did not hesitate to express nationalist sentiments. With the rise of PLO influence, censorship increased, until, during Milson's efforts to eliminate PLO sentiment, prevailing political tendencies were practically eliminated from the press. The pro-Jordanian newspaper, *al-Quds,* tended to be less critical than *al-Fajr* and *al-Sha'b.* During 1981–1982, censorship and stoppage of publication increased significantly and Arab journalists were either jailed or placed under house arrest on several occasions. The crackdown on nationalists during 1982 led to a ban on the use of "Palestine" by the Palestine News Agency.

TABLE 3

Background Information on the June 1983 Al-Bayader Assiyasi Opinion Poll

JOB DISTRIBUTION IN THOSE CONTRIBUTING TO THE POLL

Job:	Labourers	Students	Professionals	Clergies
Number:	106	125	202	37
Percentage:	13.64	16.09	26.00	4.76

Job:	Employees	Teachers	Farmers
Number:	171	89	47
Percentage:	22.01	11.45	6.05

AGE DISTRIBUTION IN THE POLL

Age (years):	Below 20	20-29	30-39	40-49	Over 50
Number:	71	225	245	181	55
Percentage:	9.14	28.96	31.53	23.30	7.07

SEX DISTRIBUTION OF THE CONTRIBUTORS

Male: 626   (80.57%)
Female: 151   (19.43%)

Total: 777   (100.00%

GEOGRAPHICAL DISTRIBUTION OF THE CONTRIBUTORS TO THE POLL

Region	Number	Percentage
Middle Region (West Bank)	271	34.88
Northern Region (West Bank)	191	24.58
Southern Region (West Bank)	232	29.86
Gaza Strip	83	10.68
TOTAL:	777	100.00

LEVEL OF EDUCATION OF CONTRIBUTORS

Education	Number	Percentage
Elementary	85	10.94
Secondary	263	33.85
University	385	49.55
Illiterates	44	5.66
TOTAL:	777	100.00

PLACE OF RESIDENCE OF CONTRIBUTORS

Place	Number	Percentage
Cities	324	41.70
Villages	295	37.97
Refugee Camps	158	20.33
TOTAL:	777	100.00

Source: Al-Bayader Assiyasi, June 1983.

Education

The education system in the West Bank has been a principal means of maintaining cohesiveness of the Arab community; it too has been subjected to the stresses and strains of occupation. The organization and patterns of education continue much as they were during the pre-1967 era, but subject to Israeli supervision. The three types of schools are private, UNRWA, and government (financed since 1967 by Israel). Education is compulsory for nine years and is free through the secondary level. All use the Jordanian curriculum. Standards and policies are coordinated to some extent by a centralized committee, the only centralized Arab organization in the West Bank. With funds provided by the Military Government, an Israeli bureau is responsible for the system. The Israeli Ministry of Education reviews the approval of textbooks, syllabuses and exams, the appointment, dismissal, and transfer of teachers and ancillary personnel, and oversees school maintenance and budgets. Although the Israeli government removed Jordanian control over schools and teachers after 1967, many teachers continued to receive salaries from Amman.

During the first years of occupation, there was a bitter controversy between the Israeli authorities and the West Bank school system over textbooks. Initially the Israel Committee of Directors-General dealing with West Bank policies, decided to introduce textbooks used by Israel's Arab school system. When this proposal was resisted by local teachers, the Jordanian curriculum was continued, but all passages deemed "inflammatory" by the Israelis were expunged. Israel maintained that the continued use of these texts was "a clear contravention of UNESCO conventions." Military Government censorship of textbooks also aroused criticism among intellectuals and university personnel within Israel, and the issue was discussed at length in the Israeli press and by Israeli civil rights organizations.

With intensification of Israeli attempts to crush pro-PLO sentiment on the West Bank, the schools became principal centers of opposition to the occupation. Student demonstrations and strikes and charges by the security authorities that pupils belonged to Palestinian organizations, assembled illegally, distributed subversive leaflets, organized violence, and agitated against the government, led to frequent disruptions. Hundreds of students were arrested yearly, with detention ranging from two days to twelve years.

The four West Bank universities were also focal points of opposition to the occupation, and also suffered disruptions resulting from curfews, student arrests, intrusions by the army, and conflicts with the Israeli authorities over textbooks and university policies. The universities, two secular and two religious, were established after 1967, two of them from secondary or preparatory schools that existed before the occupation. By 1980-81 their total enrollment was over 6,000 with a faculty of 374. Most students are male with a significant minority of women and Christians. Most of the Christians attend either Bir Zeit (secular) or Bethlehem (Freres-Catholic). Only Muslims attend the Islamic College in Hebron.

Other post-secondary institutions include a Women's Teacher Training Institute at Ramallah established by Jordan, the UNRWA Men's Teacher Training Institute in Kalandia, near Jerusalem, and several other vocational-type schools.

Health

Overall health conditions have improved since 1967, with a decrease in epidemics and a lower rate of infant mortality (28.3 per 1,000 live births in 1980). About half of all health services are provided by local charitable organizations, and half by UNRWA (for refugees) and the Military Government. Israeli authorities have assisted in expanding health training programs for nurses and paramedical technicians, in extending immunization programs, in improving sanitation systems, and in other health service improvements.

New health care insurance plans were introduced in 1973 and 1978 by Israel providing free service in all agencies and areas of the West Bank.

By March 1981, nearly 300,000 West Bank residents were covered by health insurance. The largest hospitals, nearly all in urban areas, are run by charitable societies. To serve residents of smaller towns and villages who are unable to reach the cities, charitable societies have established rural medical clinics.[16]

Despite the overall improvement of health services and conditions, some visiting international commissions, such as those sent by the WHO, have asserted that West Bank health services are still inadequate.

Relief Activities

The UNRWA establishment in the West Bank provides major services in education, health, social welfare, etc., for a substantial part of the population and has been influential in setting standards, training a body of skilled technical and administrative personnel, and in maintaining the cohesiveness of the refugee population. By 1984 more than 350,000 of the 700,000 West Bank inhabitants were registered with UNRWA as refugees. About a quarter of the refugee population lived in twenty UNRWA camps. In some areas UNRWA services were superior to those in the non-UNRWA sector. For example, refugees were generally better educated as a group than the rest of the population.[17]

Through UNRWA's assistance, thousands of poor shelters in many refugee camps were replaced and living conditions improved through self-help projects such as black-topping roads, drainage, school repairs, construction of youth centers and playgrounds. UNRWA's outpatient clinics have offered general and specialized treatment of tuberculosis, cardiovascular, opthalmic, rheumatic, and ear, nose and throat problems. UNRWA's vocational schools for young men and women have trained technicians with valuable skills required in developing economic infrastructure and many of the graduates have found job opportunities in the Gulf and in other Arab countries. Thousands of teachers who have graduated from UNRWA'S teacher training institutes have also provided needed skills across the Arab world. When the time comes to develop the economic infrastructure of the West Bank, this cadre of UNRWA teachers, physicians, social workers, skilled technicians, and administrators will be an invaluable resource.

West Bank personnel have also been trained in other charitable and relief organizations, both indigenous and foreign. Among the local groups are: Arab Children's Home Society (Jerusalem), Arab Ladies Society (Jerusalem), Arab Society for the Blind (Jerusalem), Arab Women's Federation (Beit Sahur, Bethlehem, Nablus, Taulkarm), Birzeit Ladies Charitable Society, *In'ash al-'Usrah society* (al-Bireh), Islamic Charitable Society (Hebron), Ladies' Society for Child Care (Beit Jala), Red Crescent Society (Jenin, Jerusalem, Hebron), and Society of University Graduates (Jerusalem).

The Federation of Charitable Societies coordinates a wide variety of social service and welfare activities in the West Bank including schools, orphanages, health centers, senior citizen centers, family planning centers, vocational education programs, etc.

A variety of non-Palestinian voluntary associations and societies also operate in the West Bank, assisting the population in cultural, social, economic and legal affairs. They include groups such as the American Friends Service committee (Quakers), Near East Council of Churches Committee for Refugee Work, International Committee of the Red Cross, CARE, Pontifical Missions, Baptist Hospital, Mennonite Central Committee, American Near East Refugee Aid, Lutheran World Federation, American Save the Children Federation/Community Development Foundation, AMIDEAST, and the U.N. Development Programme (UNDP). After 1977 several of these organizations met increasing difficulty in their West Bank operations because of interference by the Military Government authorities, which sought to direct the flow of assistance or to shape it to conform with Israeli policies. Consequently, many of the voluntary agencies experienced delays in obtaining the necessary Israeli approval for projects or in obtaining the permits required for personnel placement.

With establishment of the NUG in 1984 the Peres government indicated to U.S. Secretary of State George Shultz that the Military Government authorities would ease restrictions they had placed on voluntary agencies as part of the program intended to "improve the quality of life." One indication of a more lenient approach was permission granted to American and West Bank Arab investors for investigating possibilities of joint enterprises in the West Bank.

Notes

1. Much of the demographic data in this section are from J. Ishaq and C. Smith, *Demography of the Palestinians, Part One, The West Bank,* mimeo., Bethlehem University, Bethlehem, West Bank, 1982; also, Benvenisti, *The West Bank Data Project,* mimeo., 1982.

2. Bassem Abed, op. cit.

3. Benvenisti, op. cit., 1982, p. 4.

4. Ibid., p. 5.

5. Ishaq and Smith, op. cit., p. 53.

6. Ann Lesch, *Political Perceptions of the Palestinians in the West Bank and the Gaza Strip,* Washington, D.C. 1980, p. 53.

7. Ibid., p. 67.

8. Ibid., p. 75.

9. JP, August 12, 1983.

10. Richard Dekmejian, "Islamic Fundamentalism in the West Bank," unpublished survey, 1983.

11. Emile A. Nakleh, unpublished survey of West Bank political life, 1983.

12. Ibid.

13. Ibid.

14. Text of Hussein-Arafat agreement in *The New York Times,* February 24, 1985; reprinted in Appendix IV.

15. Emile Nakleh, op. cit.

16. Israel Ministry of Defense, *Judea-Samaria and the Gaza District: A Sixteen-Year Survey (1967–1983),* November 1983, pp. 27–31.

17. U.N. General Assembly, *Report of the Commissioner-General of the United Nations Relief and Works Agency for Palestine Refugees in the Near East 1 July 1983–30 June 1984,* 39th Session, supp. no. 13 (A/39/13).

8

West Bank Economy

General Observations[1]

Conclusions about the economic consequences of Israel's occupation are among the most controversial aspects of the dispute over the West Bank. The Israeli government maintains that: "Since 1967 economic life in the area has been characterized by rapid growth and a very substantial increase in living standards, made possible by the interaction of the economies of the areas with that of Israel. Economic development has proceeded without the jolting dislocations that might have been expected from the drastic political change that occurred in 1967."[2] Critics of Israel's policies maintain that because of its efforts to integrate the economy of the West Bank, Israel's high inflation has been exported to the region, that the improvement of living standards is minor, that the cost of living has risen rapidly due to equalization of prices and that without the remittances sent by Palestinians working abroad, living standards would have declined rather than improved. Israel's use of the three factors of production—land, labor and capital—in the West Bank have benefited it far more than any advantage received by Arab inhabitants of the West Bank from the occupation. Benvenisti has characterized the economy of the West Bank "as undeveloped, non-viable, stagnant and dependent. It is an auxiliary sector of both the Israeli and the Jordanian economies."[3]

In Part I it was shown that during the period of Jordanian control of the West Bank from 1949 to 1967 the area overcame the economic setback suffered as a result of separation from mandatory Palestine during the first Arab-Israel war. Despite many discriminatory policies of the Jordanian government, the economies of East and West were integrated. Severance of the West Bank from Jordan in 1967 again led to reorientation of the economy, this time from east to west, under the tutelage of a new master, with completely different economic objectives, plans, and policies than those which had prevailed for nearly twenty years. Many of these plans and objectives, as they pertain to Israel and

Jewish settlement have been analyzed above. A discussion of their impact on the indigenous Arab inhabitants follows.

The 1967 war caused a sharp decline in the level of short-run economic activity. Initially, economic ties with Jordan were severed, but they were gradually restored in accordance with Defense Minister Dayan's "open bridges" policy. During the change in administration, there was a temporary contraction in sources of employment and income, for both the Jordanian civilian administration and the army had played an important role in the economy before 1967. The uncertainty and instability immediately after the war caused a sharp cutback in investments, contributing to a slowdown of the economy.

The extensive emigration of those in the most productive ages during and immediately after the war resulted in sharp reductions of the labor force and in the size of the local market. Large scale unemployment was short-lived because emigration had reduced the "excess supply" of labor, particularly in the services branch. Furthermore emigration, by reducing the West Bank market made agricultural exports available for the East Bank, which now had a larger market for agricultural produce resulting from the new refugee influx. Agricultural produce from the West Bank now found markets not only in the East, but within Israel and in Europe via Israeli marketing arrangements.

To maintain stability in the West Bank the Israeli government sought to promote economic recovery in two fields. It initiated projects to promote employment and it hired numerous public service workers, thereby absorbing in part the economic activities of the previous Jordanian administration. Some were "make-work" labor-intensive projects such as road building, later replaced by capital-intensive projects when the labor supply decreased. Secondly, Israel provided valuable technical assistance and resources for agricultural development. This included both educational programs and direct investment in agricultural development. The pace of economic integration between Israel and the West Bank was already evident by 1970.

Some three-quarters of the merchandise trade of the administered areas was with or through Israel, compared with less than two-thirds in 1968. Income from work in Israel accounted for about 15 percent of total national product, as against only 3 percent in 1968. In 1968–70 such income accounted for 37 percent of the product increment in the areas. Residents working in Israel provided more than one-third of the total rise in Israeli employment in 1970.[4]

The shift in economic orientation from Jordan toward Israel was reflected in structural changes in agriculture and in employment. As ties with

Israel were strengthened, those with Jordan weakened, evident in the steep decline of trade over the Jordan River bridges. Although economic development has been rapid since the end of the 1960s, it has been uneven as seen in a comparison of the period from 1970-75 with the period between 1975-80. Until the mid-1970s, GNP rose rapidly, at an average of 14 percent a year. Thereafter, the increase was at a more moderate 7 percent. During the first period the growth rate of gross domestic product (gross national product less income from work outside the West Bank) rose 12 percent a year, then dipped to 7 percent during the late 1970s. This continued into the 1980s and there now appears to be stagnation in the economy. These differences correspond with demographic changes in which population increased at an annual average of 1.7 percent during the first half of the decade, but declined to 1.1 percent in the second half. The slowdown in population growth was a factor of emigration which rose from 3.6 percent per thousand in the early 1970s to 19.6 per thousand in the late 1970s. The rise in emigration coincided with reduction of employment opportunity in Israel during an era when the demand for skilled and semiskilled labor in neighboring Arab countries increased.

Absorption of West Bank labor in the Israeli market was the main factor in the vigorous development until 1975. By 1974 a third of those employed in the West Bank worked in Israel, and their wages constituted some 30 percent of the added resources available for local uses between 1970 and 1975. The rapid growth of Israel's economy between 1967 and 1973 made it possible to easily absorb the labor surpluses of the West Bank. Open unemployment was nearly eliminated by 1971, and disguised unemployment, which had been mostly in agriculture, disappeared by 1974. Labor force rates of participation reached their peak in 1974 while the gap in wages between employment in Israel and in the West Bank gradually diminished.

When Israel's economy began its descent into recession during 1973, West Bank workers who were the last hired were the first fired, although labor from the occupied areas (West Bank and Gaza) later tended to stabilize at about 8 percent. The beginning of the recession in Israel corresponded with the expansion of economic development in Jordan and other Arab countries which provided employment for thousands of West Bank temporary emigrants. Some Israeli economists cited these developments as the beginning of an integrated labor market in which West Bank Arabs would gravitate toward areas according to market place demands.

Substantial differences were created in the living patterns of West Bank Arab workers in Israel, who continued to live and to work part-time in their West Bank places of residence, and those, primarily skilled, workers who flowed to the Arab labor markets. The former maintained close contacts with their families and West Bank society whereas the emigrants to Arab countries were cut off from regular family ties, some of them unable to return at all, or infrequently, thus living more or less in limbo while their families often remained without a male head-of-household.

Economic trends in the West Bank do not fit the model of a "typical" development process in which the share of domestic consumption drops in proportion to the increase in the share of private investment. Consumption fell in the West Bank from 81 to 72 percent of total resources between 1971 and 1980, with a rise in investment from 8 to 22 percent. But unlike the typical development pattern, the increase in West Bank investment flowed into private construction, with little into nonresidential capital formation. Nor was there a decline in the weight of primary sectors of the economy (agriculture, quarrying) and an increase in industry. Agriculture still dominated the economy, providing 35 percent of domestic product in 1980, about the same as in 1970. During this period the contribution of industry actually declined from 9.5 percent in 1970 to 6.5 percent in 1980, although construction, primarily residential, increased from 6.3 to 12.5 percent.

The merging of small economic units into larger ones, another common characteristic of growth, has not occurred in the West Bank. The number of enterprises increased but their size did not. A survey of some 2,587 enterprises revealed that 1,487 workshops and factories employed fewer than three workers and only seven plants had more than 100, a situation that remained unchanged after 1967. Although this may reflect a preference for single ownership, it is more likely that growth is constrained by lack of credit facilities and capital markets as well as by Israel government restrictions on infrastructure development that could lead to industrialization.[5]

The level of physical capital formation has remained low, but there has been a high level of human capital development during the 1970s. School enrollment, starting from a relatively high level in 1970, has risen, and more students are staying in the West Bank to complete both secondary and college level work. The educational level is constantly rising among the working population with a decline in the proportion of those without schooling. The proportion of those with no education fell from 48 percent in 1970 to 37 percent in 1975 and to 29 percent in 1980. Most graduates of higher educational institutions usually have to leave the West Bank to find employment.

Private consumption patterns, tied to disposable income use, rose at an average of 10 percent a year during the first half of the 1970s but slowed to 6 percent a year in the late 1970s. The rate of savings also rose in the beginning of the decade, then declined. With the rise of expenditures on household items, 80 percent of all West Bank households have electricity for all or part of the day. By 1981 the region as a whole consumed six times as much power as in 1968. Electricity supply, formerly provided by small local generators, is now hooked up to Israel's national power grid in many areas.

There is also a substantial increase in ownership of durable goods. In 1980 there were some 38,000 autos in the West Bank compared to fewer than 7,500 in 1968. Ownership of electric or gas ranges increased from 5 percent in 1967 to 75.3 percent in 1981, of refrigerators from 5 to 51.1 percent, and of television sets from 2 to 60.7 percent. Some observers attribute the increased use of household durables to investment patterns giving preference to these items rather than to investment in industry, agriculture, etc.[6]

A substantial increase of investment in private housing began in 1974 when workers began to be laid off in Israel. Much of the private construction appeared to be undertaken by family groups, after working hours, or when demands for labor were low. Local authorities expressed concern about the problems of monitoring construction since much of it occurred without permits, on a casual basis, when either time or money is available. There was also a noticeable increase in store front structures that could or could not be used for commercial purposes. Such buildings do not necessarily increase the overall economic productivity of the community. Local residents freely admitted their reluctance to invest in commercial development because of political instability.

Public sector expenditures and consumption, already low, have continued to decline. Municipal expenditures are not likely to increase substantially because that would require an increase of direct taxation. Many services normally provided by the public sector elsewhere are provided by nonprofit organizations in the West Bank. They include UNRWA—still one of the major sources of education, social welfare, and health services—ANERA and AMIDEAST, which receive assistance from the U.S. Agency for International Development for projects in agriculture, education, and social services. The Community Development Fund and Catholic Relief Service also receive major U.S. AID funding.

Since the 1967 war, when Jordanian banks closed their doors, there has been a banking vacuum in the West Bank. Jordanian banks refused to resume operations under Israeli occupation despite invitations to do so from the Military Government. Nor was there any central monetary authority. All public sector monetary activity is financed from local income and transfers from the Israel government, although such transfers often depend on political conditions. Two Israeli banks have operated in the region, the Bank of Israel and the Israel Discount Bank, but they are not authorized to operate with the Jordanian dinar which is still legal tender in the West Bank. Money changers and local insurance agents have therefore operated a "shadow" banking system in dinars. In 1985 the Peres government indicated that an Arab bank might be opened in Nablus.

Agriculture: Changing Patterns[7]

There has been an increase in Agriculture's share of the GNP since 1967, but a decline in the percentage of the work force employed in farming. Until June 1967 agriculture provided about 24 percent of the GNP, but increased by the 1980s to about a third. The work force in agricuture declined from about 45 percent in 1967 to about a third (there are no precise figures; they vary even among official sources). Reasons for the rise in income and decline in work force include reduction of available farm land due to expansion of Israeli settlement activity; smaller size of farm units; and the modernization of agricultural methods (mechanization, better pest control, irrigation, fertilization, etc.) resulting in doubled field crops, orchard fruits and vegetables.

Immediately after the 1967 war Israel encouraged efforts to rehabilitate the agricultural sector. Within a week farmers were permitted to harvest the 1966–67 bumper crops, wells were again in use, and many employees of the Jordanian Department of Agriculture were back at their jobs. There was soon an influx of Israeli agricultural experts with advice on improving plant varieties and cultivation methods. New crop strains were introduced, improved methods of cultivation and use of chemical fertilizers were encouraged. Dairy herds were also improved.

A crop planning program instituted in 1968 encouraged farmers to change from production of high-water content produce such as watermelons or leguminous crops to reduce West Bank dependence on markets in Jordan and Arab countries to the East. Preservable crops including beans, sesame and cotton were introduced for export through Agrexco (the Israel Agricultural Export Company) as an alternative to traditional markets. Labor intensive crops were also encouraged, to absorb manpower.

By the early 1970s when West Bank unemployment declined as a result of labor export to Israel, there was a shortage of hands among West Bank farmers. Many of them, unable to compete with the high wages paid in Israel (double the wages paid on the West Bank) were forced to abandon their farms, or leave them to wives and children so the men could find work in Israel. Large farm owners often sought to return to traditional crops requiring the least labor. Israel's agricultural advisors now modified their plans and began a program to integrate Israeli and West Bank agriculture. Early efforts included educational and training programs and extension services. By the 1970s as the Israeli economy began to deteriorate, the government cut back on extension services, training and development programs, the number of long-term Agriculture Department workers and the Department budgets.

Increases in crop production were limited by the small area irrigated, only 5 to 6 percent, despite introduction of improved crop strains and better use of fertilizer. Production in the West Bank is determined by two indicators: annual rainfall and olive yield. Crop yields fluctuate because of their dependence on timing and volume of rain. Weather cycles are reinforced by the two-year cycles in the yield of olive trees. With a third of the cultivated area in olive trees, the success of the crop weighs heavily in the determination of overall production. The industrial sector is also influenced by the olive crop because of the large number of olive presses and other related processing industries such as soap.

The output of the agricultural sector increased at an average annual rate of about 8 percent until the end of the 1970s. It is difficult to estimate the extent to which this growth was a result of Israeli policies. It is also unclear whether shifts in crop cultivation intended to save labor were successful, because labor-intensive crops such as sesame were introduced at the same time to exploit the lower wage structure of the West Bank. Less produce is now marketed because of the shift in crops to serve family needs on farms where the males found work in Israel and the women and children assumed the field work. There are no records of "secondary employment" or work on farms by males returning from salaried jobs in Israel. Overall, there seems to be an increase in yields and in total production; labor utilization has decreased in comparison to output and in relation to land usage.

Future prospects for West Bank agriculture are uncertain. Although the number of tractors and combines has increased two or three times since 1967, there is a shortage of capital for further technological progress. Efforts could be made to increase the size of farms, a process necessitating land reform laws. Establishment of cooperatives might help to develop some benefits of larger holdings. The lack of credit availability could be overcome by organizations similar to the Jordanian Agricultural Credit Corporation or the credit co-ops of the Jordan Central Cooperative Union. Expansion of irrigation is now impeded by shortage of credit and the strict limits Israel places on extending water sources by withholding permits for new wells to be drilled. Many Arab wells have been confiscated by the Israeli authorities, especially in the Jordan Valley, to preserve underground water for Israeli wells in the Jordan Valley and along the coastal plain. Israel's control of the flow of goods into and out of the West Bank has influenced the free market and placed West Bank products at a disadvantage against heavily subsidized Israeli products. Permission for establishing new marketing centers and better processing facilities has been denied even when funds for these projects were available from voluntary agencies.

Industry: Little Change[8]

Generally industry has stagnated. There has been little change in its status since 1967. Israeli policy does not aim at encouraging this sector. Industry's share of the GNP has remained between 6 and 8 percent since 1967; in 1980 it used 16.8 percent of the labor force (22.3 percent was employed in construction and 34.7 percent in "other").

Industrial production is largely confined to supply of essential goods such as food processing, beverages, tobacco processing, textiles, clothing and furniture. Most production is in small workshops with modest capital. Owners and their families provide most labor, with hired help at a minimum. There were only seven firms with more than 100 employees in 1979, all established before 1967. A significant part of the labor intensive industry is subcontracting for Israeli enterprises, which keeps the Arab worker dependent on contractors. However, subcontracting has made possible a substantial increase of women in the labor force, especially in textiles and clothing.[9]

The olive crop is a major factor in the volume of industrial as well as agricultural production. Both industrial employment and production tend to fluctuate in tandem with the two-year cycle of olive production. Volume of olive production also depends on demand in Israel and to a lesser extent in Jordan.

Average labor productivity increased at an annual rate of some 12 percent between 1970 and 1976. While the number of production firms has increased since the late 1970s, the greatest aggregate increase in output was in 1969. Thereafter output began to decline.

Food, plastics and quarrying offer the highest industrial wages. There is little difference between the wages paid in Israel and in the West Bank to these laborers. This reflects the higher capital intensity in these three businesses. The wage gap in other local industries such as leather, wood, textiles and metals can be attributed partly to the large number of apprentices and women employed. They are mostly small workshops which employ the owner, his family and a few apprentices. The large number of women employed in textiles probably accounts for the low wages paid in that sector.[10]

The absence of Arab banking facilities for credit and financial transactions is a major reason for the lag in industrial development. Few
entrepreneurs have confidence in the two Israeli banks or their 28
branches in the West Bank and they are little used compared to the
Arab banks before 1967. West Bank residents have access to banks in
Amman, either directly or through money changers who mediate with
Amman and carry out transactions within the West Bank. The constant
devaluation of Israeli currency in contrast to the stability of the dinar,
which has maintained a fixed change rate since 1975, has led to the
general use of the dinar as legal tender. However, no interest is paid
on dinar deposits; rather, they require payment of a commission. Current
cash transactions are therefore handled by money changers and Amman
is used for long-term deposit of profits and savings, creating a flow of
capital to the East Bank. There is little data on the cash flow of currency
across the Jordan Bridges, but it is generally acknowledged to be
considerable. Additional cash flows into the West Bank come from
exports to Jordan and beyond, remittances from workers abroad, wages
paid by Jordan to its employees in the West Bank, and payments from
UNRWA. Israel's 1977 exchange rate reform permitting residents to
deposit their money in foreign currency accounts was also applied in
the West Bank, thus foreign currency amounted to more than half the
West Bank deposits by the end of 1980, but even this did not induce
expanded bank activity.[11]

The full flow of Israeli commodities into the West Bank may be
difficult to measure because this trade has taken on the characteristic
of internal commerce. West Bank production is not protected from
import of Israeli manufactures which move freely into the area. Residents
may import only those foreign goods approved by Israel. Many items
produced at lower cost in Israel have a comparative advantage over the
same item produced in the West Bank. Consequently, Israeli exports
to the West Bank accounted for about a quarter of all Israeli exports
in 1980.

Jordan also imposes export restrictions on goods from the West Bank.
There has been a rise in industrial exports but they are subject to
increased restrictions. Only items from enterprises established before
the 1967 war and which use raw materials purchased in Jordan can be
sent across the bridges. These restrictions, in addition to the duties
placed by Israel on all imports, impose a severe strain on the West
Bank export market. The chief items exported to Jordan are building
stone (demand has increased recently as a result of Jordan's building
boom) and certain basic food products including *samneh* (distilled grease
made from butter or lamb fat), dairy products and olive oil.

The Israeli government, like the Jordanian government before it, has invested little in infrastructure for industry (construction, electricity, training). The road system has been greatly extended and improved, largely for Israeli security needs. Several small villages were linked to the power system and road network, and in the early 1970s special training programs were developed to supply labor for certain jobs in the Israeli economy. Most of these efforts were phased out with time. With the onset of Israel's recession, most training programs were halted; now only those provided by voluntary agencies are operating.

Future prospects are constrained by other factors. Domestic markets in the West Bank are limited by low purchasing power, lack of expertise, and an unwillingness to invest capital. Much of the technology is outdated and because of the small size of firms, there is little likelihood of change. There are no complimentary services, only a primitive infrastructure, natural resources are sparse. Overriding all these limitations is political uncertainty about the future of the West Bank.

To the extent that there is limited industrial development, it will occur in existing industries such as food processing. Farming has already shifted to production of crops for canning, although a West Bank canning industry would find it difficult to compete with the highly developed and efficient canning industry in Israel.

Industries which appear to have some prospect for future development, include building stone, pharmaceuticals and furniture. None of these is likely to result in large factories, but there is room for small establishments. Certain West Bank products could have a comparative advantage over other Arab countries, either because of production methods or particular taste preferences (for example, chocolates, *samneh,* heavier olive oil). Jerusalem is still the major trading center for the West Bank but efforts to further develop markets there have been thwarted by the military administration. Amman is the entree to the rest of the Arab world, but further development of that market also depends on the future political status of the West Bank and particularly on the relationship of the area with Jordan.

Foreign Trade

With a trend of increasing dependence since 1967, Israel has become the principal source of West Bank imports and the chief market for its exports. In 1978 Israel provided 86 percent of West Bank imports, rising to 88 percent in 1980 and remaining at that level into 1982; 54 percent of West Bank exports were to Israel in 1978, 60 percent in 1980 and 54 percent in 1982. Jordan is the second largest trading partner taking 46 percent of exports in 1982 but providing only 2 percent of imports.[12] Despite long-term Israeli plans to develop an export market for West Bank agricultural commodities, only about one percent is shipped to countries other than Israel and Jordan. The West Bank has become Israel's largest export market because Israeli products are protected against competition from other sources. More industrial than agricultural products are exported from the area to Israel, but agricultural exports to Jordan are double industrial products. Industrial goods comprise about 85 percent of total imports but only 65 percent of exports. The comparison with industry's share of the domestic product is interesting, about a quarter of the value of domestic agricultural product.

Until the economic slowdown in Israel after the mid-1970s West Bank trade with Israel rose rapidly. In recent years the industrial share of exports to Jordan has increased, despite a growing number of restrictions. Accelerated growth in Jordan has been beneficial for the West Bank, and there is a correspondence between the rate of Jordan's growth and its total commodity imports from the West Bank. Traditional food items still provide about half the total value of all exports to Jordan *(samneh,* dairy products and olive oil).

The overall trade balance is adverse, offset by earnings from tourism in the West Bank, remittances from workers abroad, earnings from workers in Israel, disbursement from international relief organizations, military government expenditures, and payments received from Jordan and other Arab governments.

UNRWA is a major asset. Its expenditures for schools, vocational institutions, medical and food supplies, and salaries paid to several thousand UNRWA teachers and other employees are a major source of earnings. In 1980 UNRWA transfers to the West Bank and Gaza were estimated at some $40 million.

U.S. AID and private welfare services operating in the West Bank spend some $20 million a year. A substantial part of the AID funding is through private organizations including ANERA and AMIDEAST. It is believed that several Muslim welfare organizations receive funding from Muslim countries, although it is difficult to substantiate either the fact or the amount.

The West Bank provides both Israel and Jordan with a major source of cheap labor. Jordan receives a substantial amount of its agricultural imports from the West Bank. For Israel it is a protected market for industrial and consumer goods (about 25 percent of all Israeli exports), and is a cheap subcontracting source for labor intensive products. The "open bridges" policy has enabled Israel to export many items to Jordan and the rest of the Arab world through the West Bank, thus circumventing the Arab boycott.

Notes

1. Most of the material in this chapter is from a working paper prepared by Vivian Bull.

2. Israel Ministry of Defense, *Coordinator of Government Operations in Judea-Samaria Gaza District Sinai. A fourteen year Survey (1967–1981)*, April 1, 1982, p. 3.

3. Benvenisti, 1982, op. cit. p. 20.

4. Israel Government, *The Economy of the Administered Areas, 1970*, Jerusalem, 1971, p. 5.

5. Benvenisti, 1982, op. cit., p. 20.

6. Compiled from various sources including Israel Central Bureau of Statistics, *Statistical Abstract of Israel 1982;* Raphael Meron, *Economic Development in Judea-Samaria and the Gaza District, 1970–80,* Bank of Israel Research Department, Jerusalem, 1983; Benvenisti, 1982.

7. From working paper by Vivian Bull.

8. Ibid.

9. See Hisham Awartami, *A Survey of Industries in the West Bank and Gaza Strip,* Birzeit University, September 1979.

10. Raphael Meron, 1983, op. cit.; also Meron, *The Economy of the Administered Areas 1977–1978,* Bank of Israel, Jerusalem, 1980.

11. Ibid.

12. Benvenisti, 1982, op. cit., p. 12.

The West Bank and Middle East Politics: Some Future Options

Developments within the West Bank such as Jewish settlement activity, Arab political unrest, and the autonomy negotiations have had a wide influence on larger political trends in the Middle East. A major reason for Israel's invasion of Lebanon in 1982 was to undermine the power and influence of the PLO and to isolate the West Bank from the organization. Although Israel maintained that the influence of the PLO was based on its use of force against critics, public opinion polls in the West Bank indicated that the organization had wide popular backing. The Likud government perceived the PLO as the chief instigator of Palestinian unrest in the region and therefore was determined to eliminate its influence, not only within the West Bank, but from its principal bases of operation in Lebanon.

The invasion of Lebanon and Israel's strict military government policies in the West Bank prior to the invasion were major reasons for the slowdown, nearly to a halt, of negotiations between Egypt and Israel in the normalization process and the West Bank autonomy plan, throwing into jeopardy the accomplishments of the Egyptian-Israeli treaty and the Camp David peace process.

Jewish settlement in the West Bank and Israeli policies toward the Arab population there were among the obstacles in extending the peace negotiations to Jordan. Although provision was made for a Jordanian role in the negotiations for the 1978 Camp David agreements, King Hussein resisted participation without a signal of approval from the Palestinians, including those in the West Bank, in the leadership of the PLO, and from his own Palestinians who constitute over half of Jordan's population. Jordan has also been wary of entering the peace negotiations because of reactions from other Arab states, especially Saudi Arabia and Syria.

Saudi Arabia has been concerned with developments in the West Bank because of its interest in Jerusalem, considered by its rulers as an Islamic holy site next in importance to Mecca and Medina, because of Saudi financial support to the Palestinians including assistance to West Bank welfare projects as well to the PLO, and because the Saudis perceive the outcome of negotiations on the future of the West Bank and Jerusalem as a key to solution of the Arab-Israeli conflict. The Saudis regard the U.S. position on the West Bank in relation to issues such as Jewish settlement, as a touchstone of American balance in relations with the Arabs and Israel.

For Syria, the future of the Golan Heights is more important than the West Bank. However, West Bank attitudes toward the PLO are important for Syria because of its desire to control the Palestinian organizations and to determine their political course.

Other Arab states also perceive events in the West Bank and policies of governments such as the U.S. toward the area as a touchstone in relations between Israel and the Arabs. Some observers maintain that American support for Israel on issues such as Jewish settlement and other similar controversial questions, will be interpreted by Arab governments as a sign of strength and U.S. determination to maintain a strong Israel. Others believe that such American support will undermine U.S. credibility with Arab governments and weaken relations with them.

The uncertainties of current Middle East political trends and the role of the West Bank in them are underscored by the perilous position of Arafat and his supporters in their struggle with Syria. Until recently Arafat and the PLO were considered to be the unqualified representatives of the Palestinians including those in the West Bank. Recent events have thrown this representation into question and have raised doubts about future political representation among West Bank Palestinians, their willingness to participate in the autonomy negotiations, and the role of Jordan in these negotiations.

The Future of the West Bank

Many Middle East specialists perceive the future of the West Bank as the key to a resolution of the Arab-Israel conflict. It will determine: (1) the credibility of American policy in the region; (2) the willingness of Israel and the Arab states to reach compromises on an issue of major importance to both sides; and (3) the degree to which Palestinian political aspirations will be realized, thus diminishing, in proportion to fulfillment of these aspirations, the regional instability caused by Palestinian uprootedness.

Options for the future of the West Bank range from (1) its incorporation into Israel as an integral part of the Jewish state, (2) to its establishment as an independent Palestinian Arab state. Diverse intermediate options include (3) the Camp David autonomy plan, (4) federation or confederation with Jordan, (5) a tripartite Israel-Jordan-Palestinian confederal relationship, (6) partition between Jordan and Israel, (7) shared rule between Jordan and Israel, and (8) international trusteeship.

It is unlikely that the future of the area will be determined by considerations such as the free choice of the inhabitants, economic viability, or military security. Although these may count heavily in decisions about the future, it is much more likely that the ultimate political status of the region will be based on international bargaining, the relative strength of proponents, and the degree to which the United States is willing and able to use its influence to shape the outcome. American policy regarding the West Bank, in turn, will be determined by the balance in U.S. relationships between the Arab states and Israel, domestic political considerations, and American plans for Middle East security. Each option is considered below.

Israeli Annexation

Annexation is the option most favored by the Likud bloc and other even more nationalist factions, several of them represented in the NUG. Their rationale is more ideological than security based. Their programs for Jewish settlement in the West Bank and for integrating the area (and Gaza) into Israel, although suspended, have not been thwarted. Notwithstanding widespread internal opposition to annexationist policies, if not the actual formal act of annexation, the 1977-84 Likud government progressed so far in its goal that even many of its opponents claimed that the "point of no return" had already been passed. Annexationists disregard the "demographic argument" against annexation put forward by Israeli and other Zionists who are concerned that Israel will either lose or substantially diminish its Jewish character. The nationalists point to the slowdown of growth in the Arab population of the West Bank, and prospects that a large part of that population will be encouraged to leave should the region become an integral part of Israel. The widespread opposition of the Arab inhabitants to annexationist policies has been largely contained through the use of martial law, military government, expulsion of political dissidents, and other similar measures.

Even if a Labor government freed of Likud takes office the extent to which "the point of no return" has been reached in establishment of new Jewish settlements, integration of the economic and service infrastructure, and the emotional attachments that large numbers of Israelis have for the West Bank, will make it unlikely that integrationist policies will be reversed, although they may be slowed as they were by the NUG. At the present time the only potential obstacle to the continuation of West Bank integration with Israel is an overt and forceful counter policy by the United States government. The annexationist trend may be slowed by the vigorous entry of Jordan into negotiations over the future of the West Bank. When confronted with an Arab negotiating partner, some Israelis argue, concessions are more likely to be forthcoming.

Failure to halt the process of integration would undermine revival of the Reagan plan, which calls for planning the future of the West Bank in association with Jordan. Continuation of integration would weaken U.S. relations with the Arab states. This might diminish the credibility of American policy in the Middle East and the capacity of the U.S. to be an effective intermediary in the Arab-Israel conflict. It could strengthen the militants among Arab nationalists and those who oppose compromise solutions by demonstrating U.S. inability to effectively mediate or to implement policies in the region not to Israel's liking.

Independent Palestine Arab State

Although establishment of an independent Palestinian Arab state is the option preferred by most inhabitants of the West Bank according to public opinion polls, it has been rejected by most political factions in Israel, including those in the NUG. All leading American political candidates in both the Democratic and Republican parties have also opposed this option.

On the other hand, establishment of a West Bank state is the minimum demand of the great majority of Palestinian nationalist moderates (militants insist that all of Palestine, including Israel, must become the Palestinian state). The moderate position is favored by most members of the Arab League. Exceptions include Libya which opposes a two state solution.

Israel's arguments about the threat to its security from an independent Palestine state have been countered by a variety of proposals for demilitarization and control of arms imports, and by Israel's own predominant military strength which at present surpasses that of all potentially combined hostile Arab countries.

The economic viability of an independent Palestinian state has been questioned, but the large number of independent countries with far smaller natural and human resources demonstrates that economic viability cannot be determined in absolute terms. It will be determined by potential foreign aid, the capacity of high level manpower to utilize limited resources, and other similar factors.

In any event, a West Bank–Gaza Palestinian state would be unable to absorb all four million Palestinians. Most of them would probably not want to return to Palestine. The majority of immigrants would probably be those still living in refugee camps (a total of 765,000 at the end of 1984), although not all of them might choose to return. While the West Bank would probably be able to establish a workable economic existence without a large influx of immigrants, it would require substantial international economic assistance to absorb several hundred thousand refugees.

An independent Palestinian state would face a number of political problems. It would be bordered by nations that are considerably more powerful, especially Israel and Syria, and thus would likely become the focal point of covert, if not overt, intervention by forces seeking to influence its political orientation. Possibilities are strong that Israel, Jordan and Syria would compete for influence within a new Palestinian entity. There would also be competition for political influence or control between the internal leadership, which has developed strong local institutions, and the external, returning leadership, such as the cadres of the PLO. The major advantage of an independent state is that it is the option most favored by the inhabitants of the West Bank and its implementation would considerably diminish the regional tensions arising from Palestinian homelessness.

Camp David Autonomy Plan

The Camp David autonomy plan was deliberately vague, so that it could be interpreted differently by each signatory to the agreement. The plan was included in the "Framework for Peace in the Middle East" signed at Camp David by Israel, Egypt and the U.S. on September 17, 1978 and called for negotiations on resolution of "the Palestine problem in all its aspects" between Egypt, Israel, Jordan and the representatives of the Palestinian people. The three stages of negotiations were to include:

(a) transitional arrangements for the West Bank and Gaza not to exceed five years during which there would be "a peaceful and orderly transfer of authority" from the Israeli Military Government to a status to be agreed on. Jordan would be invited to join these negotiations. To "provide full autonomy to the inhabitants, under these arrangements the Israeli military government and its civilian administration will be withdrawn as soon as a self-governing authority has been freely elected by the inhabitants of these areas to replace the existing military government." The new arrangements "should give due consideration both to the principle of self-government by the inhabitants of these territories and to the legitimate security concerns of the parties involved."

(b) Egypt, Israel and Jordan were to agree "on the modalities for establishing the elected self-governing authority in the West Bank and

Gaza." Palestinians could be included in the Egyptian and Jordanian delegations. The powers and responsibilities of the self-governing authority would be negotiated by the parties to the agreement. "A withdrawal of Israeli armed forces will take place and there will be a redeployment of the remaining Israeli forces into specified security locations" to assure security and public order, "a strong local police force will be established, which may include Jordanian citizens." Israeli and Jordanian forces would participate in maintaining security of the borders.

(c) The five-year transition period was to begin "when the self-governing authority (administrative council) in the West Bank and Gaza is established and inaugurated." Negotiations on the final status of the West Bank and Gaza and their future relationships with neighbors would begin "not later than the third year after beginning of the transitional period," and a peace treaty between Israel and Jordan would be concluded by the end of the transitional period. "The legitimate rights of the Palestinian people" and their participation "in the determination of their own future" would be assured through their participation in the negotiations, by "submitting their agreement to a vote by the elected representatives of the inhabitants of West Bank and Gaza" and by "providing for the elected representatives . . . to decide how they shall govern themselves consistent with the provisions of their agreement."

The provisions of the autonomy agreement were confirmed in a joint letter signed by President Sadat and Prime Minister Begin to President Carter accompanying the Egyptian-Israeli peace treaty of March 26, 1979, in which they agreed to begin negotiations on autonomy outlined at Camp David, within a month. Several rounds of negotiations were held, and they were broken off several times during the next few years because of Egyptian disapproval of Israeli actions such as the annexation of Jerusalem, 1978 and 1982 invasions of Lebanon, as well as by disagreements over the substance of the autonomy itself. Among the key issues in dispute between Egypt and Israel were the authority to be allocated to the proposed administrative council, who would be represented in the council and who could participate in elections for it.

The United States and Egypt perceived the outcome of the plan as some form of Palestinian self-government. Egypt perceived the plan as a transitional stage and a first step toward achieving self-determination, without excluding the possibility of a Palestinian state. While Egypt did not believe that the autonomy agreement would solve the Palestinian problem, it was regarded as a step toward an overall solution. Furthermore, Egypt's position was that autonomy would not succeed without participation of the Palestinians in the negotiations. The U.S. also regarded the autonomy plan as a first step toward solution of the conflict, however it was ambiguous about the final results, with opposition to establishment of an independent Palestinian state because of the American belief that such a state would be a volatile element, disruptive of stability in the region.

The position of the Likud government has been stated above, i.e., that autonomy was to be an intermediate step toward granting local self-government to Palestinians living in a West Bank that would become an integral part of Israel. The Labor opposition opposed this interpretation, favoring autonomy that would lead toward political integration with Jordan, but leaving security under Israeli control.

Jordan opposed autonomy although there was disagreement within the government about the future of the West Bank. King Hussein's position was to regain control of the West Bank to prevent establishment of a Palestinian state whose radical ideology might undermine the monarchy and subvert the Palestinian majority in Jordan. Rather, he favored a federation plan. The official position was willingness to accept an independent West Bank state provided it had strong links with Jordan. The Camp David version of autonomy was opposed because it excluded East Jerusalem from the negotiations, did not ban further Jewish settlements, and legitimized Israel's presence in the West Bank.

The Palestinian leadership on the West Bank opposed the plan because it did not recognize the Palestinians' right to self-determination, and because Begin openly declared that it would not permit the establishment of a Palestinian state. As with Jordan, Palestinians also complained that Camp David did not deal with Jerusalem, and gave Israel veto power over decisions of the proposed autonomy council.

Events in the region have overtaken the Camp David autonomy plan. The breakdown in negotiations between Israel, Egypt and the United States, resulting from Israel's policies in Lebanon, and the growing confrontation between West Bank nationalists and the Israeli military authorities, have so discredited the plan among the general population, that even the Village Leagues called for self-determination rather than support for Begin's version of the autonomy scheme. Finally, even if negotiations were resumed, the plan would hardly have credibility among a population strongly opposed to it. To validate this option it would be necessary for the U.S. to assure that autonomy is a temporary, intermediate program and that the West Bank population would be guaranteed a large measure of self-government at the end of the autonomy period.

Federation with Jordan

A detailed proposal for federation of the West Bank and Jordan was offered by King Hussein in 1972. Under the plan, the Hashemite Kingdom would become the United Arab Kingdom. Its two parts would be the Jordan Region and the Palestine Region, to include the West Bank and any other parts of liberated Palestine whose inhabitants desired to join. Amman would be the capital of the central government as well as the Jordan Region. East Jerusalem would be the capital of the Palestine Region. The King would be head of state and head of the central executive authority, to be assisted by a central government responsible for matters concerning the kingdom as a whole. Regional matters for each part of the kingdom would be handled by the respective executive authority in each region (Palestine and Jordan) except for matters defined by the constitution as the responsibility of the central executive authority. When first proposed, this plan was rejected by Israel, the PLO, many Palestinian inhabitants of the West Bank and by other Arab states. Had such an offer been made before 1967 when the West Bank was part of Jordan, its chances of success would probably have been much greater. During that era, federation with Jordan would have been considered by many West Bank inhabitants as an offer to share power despite opposition from some Palestinians who always opposed Hashemite rule. However, since 1967, especially during the period following the rise of the PLO after the mid-1970s, strong opposition to the Hashemite monarchy developed among Palestinian nationalists. King Hussein's repression of the PLO during 1970-71 led to decline of Jordanian influence in the West Bank and a loss of prestige among those associated with the Hashemites, as evident in the 1976 West Bank local elections.

Proposals for federation were rejected by the Likud government as inconsistent with its determination to maintain a formal Israeli presence on the West Bank, and by Labor before 1977 because it would deprive Israel of control in areas deemed essential to its security. Labor might accept a modified form of federation if combined with some version of the Allon Plan, or one of the tripartite proposals which follow. A Palestine-Jordan federation would conform with U.S. objectives for it would place the West Bank under control of a friendly and "trusted" Arab regime, provide for a larger measure of Palestinian self-government, and end the uncertainties created by Israel's rule of a large nationalistic Arab population.

Tripartite Israel-Jordan-Palestinian Confederation

This proposal combines elements of several others and could be implemented in a variety of ways—along the lines of the Allon Plan, the autonomy scheme, partial federation with Jordan, etc. No political group of consequence has adopted this plan as its own, but Labor party leader, Shimon Peres, has discussed possibilities of a regional confederation into which this scheme might fit. One asset is that it could be the basis of an economic union, or common market permitting the free exchange of goods across political frontiers. It would tend to deescalate the bitter discussion over national frontiers and security borders. The crucial question in this type of proposal is how to balance the disparity between the three proposed partners in economic development, military strength, political influence, and relationships with outside powers such as the U.S. Obviously, relationships among the three would be unequal and Israel would tend to dominate, with Jordan as the second most influential member and the Palestinians with little or no influence in major decisions.

Within Israel, the plan might be acceptable to a number of political leaders in addition to Peres. Even Begin modified his former aspiration to include all the Hashemite Kingdom within the frontiers of the Jewish state, to a goal of ultimate federation making it possible for Jews to gain access to the land across the Jordan River. This proposal is unlikely to find support with the two lesser members of the proposed confederation because of the dominant position Israel would assert in tripartite relationships. Nor would other Arab states find the plan attractive for similar reasons.

Partition of the West Bank Between Israel and Jordan

This proposal is more theoretical than practical. None of the parties to the Palestine dispute has proposed partition of the West Bank as a serious basis for a solution. Partition would create a very ambiguous situation because the parts of the region that would be demanded by Israel are those along the Jordan River, east of the heavily populated Arab sections which would be allocated to Jordan. In other words, parts of the West Bank that Jordan would receive would be cut off from the kingdom by the security belt along the Jordan River desired by Israel. Another repartition of Palestine seems to have few if any advantages for Israel, for Jordan, or for the inhabitants of the West Bank. The only plausible reason for this scheme would be to find a hasty formula. However, partition would probably lead to the rise of irredentism in Israel, among the Palestinians, and in Jordan, creating more problems than it would solve.

Shared Rule Between Jordan and Israel

A number of Israeli scholars of diverse political orientation have proposed a system of shared rule between Jordan, Israel and the Palestinians. Under this scheme local self-rule would be extended to Palestinians in the West Bank as well as in Gaza, within a framework of joint Israeli-Jordanian governance or condominium. The plan would be effected following the five year transition period called for in the Camp David autonomy scheme. While the proposers call it "the only realistic option for peace" on the agenda, it too has many of the shortcomings of the other proposed schemes. It would be difficult to implement without a peace settlement between Israel and Jordan, and would fail to satisfy the national political aspirations of the West Bank Arab population, leading to continued clashes between them and the governing authorities. An unusual amount of trust would be required between Israel and Jordan to devise a working relationship in which the two countries shared political control in an area deemed vital to each. If it has been difficult to implement the normalization process in the Israel-Egyptian peace arrangement, it would be even more difficult to normalize relations between Israel and Jordan which would tend to resent Israel's dominant position in the condominium. Nor would Jordan be able to enter this kind of relationship without at least tacit approval of the Palestinians and other Arab countries. The difficulties created for Egypt and for Lebanon with the rest of the Arab world, resulting from their unilateral agreements with Israel, demonstrate that separate peace pacts can be costly. For Jordan, the price would be even higher and it is unlikely to assume the risk, which could far exceed the benefits.

On a practical level, such an arrangement would also be highly problematic. Day-to-day issues causing vast jurisdictional disputes would, in all likelihood, doom this option in its infancy.

International Trusteeship

The 1947 U.N. Partition Plan called for an international trusteeship over Jerusalem, but it was never implemented. Neither Israel nor Jordan were willing to accept U.N. trusteeship, nor were most of the inhabitants of Jerusalem enthusiastic about it. Trusteeship for Palestine was also briefly considered by the U.S. as a temporary alternative to the partition plan in 1948 when partition was opposed by the Arab states. However, the idea was dropped as soon as Israel declared its independence in May 1948.

A trusteeship might have short-term validity as a temporary measure during the transition to a long-term solution, but in the long run it would tend to make the West Bank the focal point of diverse international tensions which have surfaced at the United Nations–East–West conflicts, Third World versus the West, Arab versus Israel, etc. All the difficulties encountered in setting up an international regime for Jerusalem would be magnified several times in attempting to establish a similar regime for the whole West Bank. Just as the residents of Jerusalem would resent imposition of some outside authority on the city, West Bank residents would also tend to regard an outside authority as "foreign rule," a modified form of occupation. Because there are few genuine "international" civil servants, the administrative personnel in an international authority would reflect the interests of their respective nations. Israel would reject international trusteeship over the West Bank because it would diminish Israeli political control, the security advantages it has gained, and because it generally tends to distrust international, especially U.N. operations in the Middle East. Rather than diminishing tensions and conflict in the West Bank, international trusteeship, in the context of present international relations, would probably greatly exacerbate unrest.

Summary of Options

A major defect of these options is that none considers the role of Jerusalem in the Arab-Israel conflict. No survey of the West Bank or consideration of proposals for its future can realistically omit Jerusalem. The city is inextricably tied to the economy, history, politics, and psychological orientation of the West Bank and its Arab population. Jerusalem has always been a dominant factor in the lives of West Bank inhabitants. Nor can the future of Gaza be separated from the West Bank. The probability is high that the fate of both regions will be determined together.

None of the options considered here will resolve the most crucial dilemma in the conflict—i.e., the apparent inconsistency between Israel's quest for security and the Palestinian Arab quest for "empowerment," or identity. Each of these quests is more psychological than substantive, quests whose outcome will be found in people's minds rather than in tangibles that can be measured quantitatively. Therefore, in postulating options, their symbolism as well as their substantive character is important. The difficulties of the incompatibility between the Israeli quest for security and Palestinian search for identity are made even more difficult by the ideological irredentism of Likud and the other nationalist parties to the right of Likud. No Israeli government can ignore or substantially diminish the growing hold "territorialist" Zionism has obtained on voters in the country.

None of the proposed territorial options can resolve the Arab refugee dilemma. The most economically advantageous Palestinian territorial entity would be unable to absorb all or most Palestinians, or even most of those who still live in refugee camps. Hundreds of thousands of Palestinians will be unable to return to the proposed Palestinian homeland. How then will such a postulated homeland diminish the volatility of the Palestinian element in the Arab-Israel conflict? It could, as did the creation of Israel for the Jews, diminish the feeling of "powerlessness" that has pervaded Palestinian consciousness since 1948, thereby lessening those attitudes that feed terrorism and Middle East instability. Can the equally difficult psychological problem of Israeli insecurity be lessened by a solution to the Palestinian dilemma? To the extent that the pressure of the Palestinian problem is eased on many areas of political sensitivity in the region (such as Lebanon), Israel's genuine insecurity will be diminished.

10

Conclusion

Major Trends and Developments, 1967–1985

1. Labor's Role: Uncertain Policies

During the first decade of Israeli control of the West Bank, the Labor Alignment was in power. It had no clear-cut or decisive policy toward the region, although it did enact legislation making Jerusalem part of Israel. Divisiveness within Labor, international pressures, and concern about integrating a large Arab population within the Jewish state restrained movement toward annexation. However, Labor did renounce a return to the pre-1967 frontiers: A new situation was created by the 1967 war in which Israel's security would be given paramount consideration as part of a peace settlement. With security as the foundation of its policy, Labor encouraged limited Jewish settlement in the West Bank, in regions approved by the government, took control of scarce resources such as water and land, and began to integrate the economic infrastructure of the region with Israel. To facilitate normalization of life for the Arab population, the West Bank was permitted access to Jordan, through the "Open Bridges" policy, assistance was given in restoration of economic activity and public functions at the municipal level, but region-wide political activity was banned; there was strict enforcement of Military Government control over the Arab inhabitants. Labor's ambiguous policies in the West Bank encouraged militant groups such as Gush Emunim to establish illicit settlements which the government found difficult to remove or control. When Labor left office in 1977, the role of the West Bank as a bargaining card for peace negotiations had diminished.

2. Likud's Role: Rapid Integration

Likud policy from 1977 until 1984 was clear-cut and decisive, with emphasis on integrating the West Bank as an integral part of Israel. This policy was motivated as much by Herut ideology, emphasizing territorial unification of the Land of Israel, as by security considerations. To hasten unification, Jewish settlement was given great encouragement and assistance by the government, by Zionist institutions, and through the private sector. There were no restrictions on areas within the West Bank where Jews could settle since the whole region was considered to be an integral part of the Jewish state. Measures to integrate West Bank infrastructure such as water systems, the electricity grid and the road network with Israel were hastened. Priority in the use of land and water was given to Jewish settlements in all parts of the West Bank where they were located. Arab opposition to Jewish settlement and plans for political absorption were dealt with more severely than under Labor and attempts were made to sever all ties between West Bank inhabitants and the Palestinian nationalist movement, especially the PLO. An attempt was made to replace Arab attraction to the PLO with establishment of rural-based Village Leagues opposed to the PLO-oriented urban leadership. Prime Minister Begin developed an autonomy plan for the Arab inhabitants of the West Bank, under the Camp David peace agreements, in which limited self-government would be extended to individuals, but would not be applicable to the territory, which would become part of Israel.

3. Israeli Public Opinion: A Divided Constituency

Israeli public opinion was sharply divided on the future of the West Bank and on Likud policies there. Many Israelis within Labor feared that integration of the region would diminish the Jewish character of Israel. On issues concerning the West Bank the spectrum ranged from Gush Emunim which opposed any restrictions on Jewish settlement and full integration into Israel, to Peace Now which called for a freeze on further settlements and negotiations with the Palestinians about the future of the area. As the Likud government facilitated development of urban settlements extending inexpensive housing and other benefits to Jewish settlers, the number who were willing to take advantage of these opportunities increased. Although opinion was divided on the political future of the West Bank, the material advantages offered to settlers seemed to undercut effective opposition to integration with Israel.

4. The West Bank under Military Government: Significant Change

The West Bank experienced greater economic, political and social change under the Israeli Military Government Administration after 1967 than at any time in the 20th Century. But better opportunities and greater economic advantages attracted skilled Palestinian workers to other countries, especially the Arab Gulf states. Thus, despite a high birth rate, the exodus of Arabs from the region resulted in little overall population increase between 1967 and 1985. However, the birth rate too, was declining due to lowered fertility rates and thus no great Arab population expansion is anticipated in the near future. Living standards have increased substantially and economic growth was rapid, but the economy of the West Bank became greatly dependent on Israel, and to a lesser extent on Jordan. Israeli development policy in the West Bank gave priority to use of scarce resources such as land and water to Jewish settlers, placing limits on extension of Arab agriculture and expansion of urban areas. Over a third of West Bank Arab workers were employed in Israel. Some observers cited remittances from expatriate workers as the chief source of economic improvement, and charged Israel with exporting its economic problems to the occupied territories. Agriculture is still an important aspect of the West Bank economy, but the percentage of the work force in farming has declined. The amount of land and water available for Arab use has also declined as a result of government policies giving priority in the use of these resources to Jewish settlements. Arab industrial development has stagnated since 1967. Overall, the economy of the West Bank has been defined by the former Deputy Mayor of Jerusalem Meron Benveniste as "undeveloped, nonviable, stagnant and dependent. It is an auxiliary sector of both the Israeli and the Jordanian economies."

5. Israel's Military Government: Control and Coercion

Israeli authorities in the West Bank have maintained tight control of Arab political and social life, preventing any major insurrection or significant disruptive activities. All political activity, the press, the curricula of educational institutions, travel, building permits, and land and water use are tightly controlled by a complex web of emergency laws and military regulations. Elections for municipal and local council offices were held in 1972 and 1976, but suspended in 1980 because of political unrest. Palestinian opposition generated a harsh government response, including increased arrests, the dismissal of elected municipal councils, and the arming of Jewish settlers. Government policies since 1977 have aimed at eliminating support for the PLO on the West Bank in two ways: (1) the destruction of the PLO's political-military infrastructure in Lebanon, seen in Israel as the source of its West Bank support, and (2) support for such non-PLO political movements on the West Bank as the Village Leagues. Few Arab inhabitants have joined these movements. However, Arab public opinion seemed to support: (a) the moderate wing of the PLO, (b) Yassir Arafat, (c) opposition to the autonomy plan, and (d) negotiations with Israel leading to a West Bank

Palestinian state coexisting with Israel. Despite the apparent divisions within the PLO, Arafat seemed to maintain support among West Bank Palestinians. Supporters of the PLO represented younger urban leaders replacing the older elites who had maintained their influence since the Ottoman era, through the British mandate, the Jordanian era and the first years of Israeli control.

6. The National Unity Government: Ambivalence

After establishment of the National Unity Government in September 1984 under Labor party leader Shimon Peres as Prime Minister, some of the more rigid controls of the previous Likud government in the West Bank were modified. Peres, at the behest of the U.S. promised to direct policy toward "improving the quality of life" for West Bank Arabs and those in the other occupied territories. This involved permitting outside and local investment in the West Bank and replacement of some Israeli Military Government officers with approved West Bank Arab officials in local offices. Peres also expressed interest in renewing discussion with Egypt about the autonomy plan and in opening negotiations with Jordan although he remained adamant in refusing to negotiate with the PLO, despite assertions from King Hussein that the Palestinian organization was prepared to recognize Israel and to conclude peace with it under the auspices of an international conference.

7. The West Bank and Middle East Politics

The future of the West Bank and the issues related to it such as Jewish settlement and Israeli control policies had an impact on the broader scope of Middle East politics. These issues affected relations between Israel and the U.S., Egypt, Jordan and other Arab countries; they were related to Israeli policy in Lebanon; and they were an integral part of the approach to a Middle East peace settlement. The failure of the Arab states and the Palestinian national movement to define a viable political framework for West Bank negotiations has contributed to the persistence of the problem. Developments over the past few years, however, particularly the actions of Jordan's King Hussein, offered room for cautious optimism that new political trends were emerging. In this period the Arab world has generally accepted the notion that the Arab-Israeli conflict and the West Bank issue must be resolved politically, not militarily. Even though specific Arab proposals have been inadequate, this is an important transition.

8. *The Search for a Solution: The U.S. Role*

Since 1967, the role of the U.S. in the search for a West Bank solution has expanded steadily. By virtue of close U.S.-Israeli ties—and the Arab perception that these ties give the U.S. substantial influence over Israel— the U.S. has become an indispensable element in West Bank discussions. Negotiating a successful resolution will require the ongoing commitment of U.S. political, economic and diplomatic resources. Moreover, in view of the importance of the West Bank in the broader peace process, the U.S. cannot afford a passive stance. The nature and extent of the U.S. commitment are also critical; the role of mediator requires vitality in the expression of new ideas and creativity in the accommodation of conflicting interests.

Appendixes

Appendix I

The Peace Plan of Israel as Presented in a Speech of Prime Minister Menachem Begin in the Knesset, December 28, 1977

Mr. Chairman, respected Knesset members, with the establishment of peace, we shall propose to introduce administrative autonomy for the Arab residents of Judea, Samaria and the Gaza District on the basis of the following principles:

1. The administration of the military government in Judea, Samaria and the Gaza district will be abolished.
2. In Judea, Samaria and the Gaza district, administrative autonomy of the Arab residents, by and for them, will be established.
3. The residents of Judea, Samaria and the Gaza district will elect an administrative council composed of 11 members. The administrative council will operate in accordance with the principles laid down in this paper.
4. Any resident, 18 years old and above, without distinction of citizenship, or if stateless, is entitled to vote in the elections to the administrative council.
5. Any resident whose name is included in the list of candidates for the administrative council and who, on the day the list is submitted, is 25 years old or above, is entitled to be elected to the council.
6. The administrative council will be elected by general, direct, personal, equal and secret ballot.
7. The period of office of the administrative council will be four years from the day of its election.
8. The administrative council will sit in Bethlehem.
9. All the administrative affairs relating to the Arab residents of the area of Judea, Samaria and the Gaza district, will be under

the direction and within the competence of the administrative council.

10. The administrative council will operate the following departments: education, religious affairs, finance, transportation, construction and housing, industry, commerce and tourism, agriculture, health, labor and social welfare, rehabilitation of refugees, and the department for the administration of justice and the supervision of the local police force, and promulgate regulations relating to the operations of these departments.

11. Security and public order in the areas of Judea, Samaria and the Gaza district will be the responsibility of the Israeli authorities.

12. The administrative council will elect its own chairman.

13. The first session of the administrative council will be convened 30 days after the publication of the election results.

14. Residents of Judea, Samaria and the Gaza district, without distinction of citizenship, or if stateless, will be granted free choice (option) of either Israeli or Jordanian citizenship.

15. A resident of the areas of Judea, Samaria and the Gaza district who requests Israeli citizenship will be granted such citizenship in accordance with the citizenship law of the state.

16. Residents of Judea, Samaria and the Gaza district who, in accordance with the right of free option, choose Israeli citizenship, will be entitled to vote for, and be elected to the Knesset in accordance with the election law.

17. Residents of Judea, Samaria and the Gaza district who are citizens of Jordan or who, in accordance with the right of free option will become citizens of Jordan, will elect and be eligible for election to the parliament of the Hashemite Kingdom of Jordan in accordance with the election law of that country.

18. Questions arising from the vote to the Jordanian parliament by residents of Judea, Samaria and the Gaza district will be clarified in negotiations between Israel and Jordan.

19. A committee will be established of representatives of Israel, Jordan and the administrative council to examine existing legislation in Judea, Samaria and the Gaza district and to determine which legislation will continue in force, which will be abolished and what will be the competence of the administrative council to promulgate regulations. The rulings of the committee will be adopted by unanimous decisions.

20. Residents of Israel will be entitled to acquire land and settle in the areas of Judea, Samaria and the Gaza districts. Arabs, residents of Judea, Samaria and the Gaza district who, in accordance with

the free options granted them, will become Israeli citizens, will be entitled to acquire land and settle in Israel.

21. A committee will be established of representatives of Israel, Jordan and the administrative council to determine norms of immigration to the areas of Judea, Samaria and the Gaza district. The committee will determine the norms whereby Arab refugees residing outside Judea, Samaria and the Gaza district will be permitted to immigrate to these areas in reasonable numbers. The ruling of the committee will be adopted by unanimous decision.

22. Residents of Israel and residents of Judea, Samaria and the Gaza district will be assured of movement and freedom of economic activity in Israel, Judea, Samaria and the Gaza district.

23. The administrative council will appoint one of its members to represent the council before the Government of Israel for deliberation on matters of common interest; and one of its members to represent the council before the Governmnet of Jordan for deliberation on matters of common interest.

24. Israel stands by its right and its claim of sovereignty to Judea, Samaria and the Gaza district. In the knowledge that other claims exist, it proposes for the sake of the agreement and the peace, that the question of sovereignty be left open.

25. With regard to the administration of the holy places of three religions in Jerusalem, a special proposal will be drawn up and submitted that will include the guarantee of freedom of access to members of all faiths to the shrines holy to them.

26. These principles will be subject to review after a five-year period. Mr. Chairman, I must now explain the 11th clause of this plan, as well as the 24th clause.

Esteemed Knesset members: In the 11th clause of our plan we postulated: The security and public order of the areas of Judea, Samaria and Gaza will be entrusted to the hands of the Israeli authorities. Without this clause there is no meaning to the plan of administrative autonomy. I wish to announce from the Knesset rostrum that this self-evidently includes deployment of IDF forces in Judea, Samaria and in the Gaza Strip.

Source: Aryeh Shalev, *The Autonomy—Problems and Possible Solutions,* Paper No. 8, Jan. 1980, Center for Strategic Studies, Tel-Aviv University. The translation was taken from: British Broadcast Corporation (B.B.C.), Survey of World Broadcasting (SWB), Middle East and North Africa, ME/5702/A/1, 30.12.77; and from: *Near East Report* (Washington), V. XXII, No. 29, July 19, 1978.

Appendix II

Sadat Plan for West Bank and Gaza, July, 1978

"Proposals relative to withdrawal from the West Bank and Gaza and Security Arrangements."

1. The establishment of a just and lasting peace in the Middle East necessitates a just solution of the Palestinian question in all its aspects on the basis of the legitimate rights of the Palestinian people and taking into consideration the legitimate security concerns of all the parties.

2. In order to ensure a peaceful and orderly transfer of authority there shall be a transitional period not exceeding five years at the end of which the Palestinian people will be able to determine their own future.

3. Talks shall take place between Egypt, Jordan, Israel and representatives of the Palestinian people with the participation of the UN with a view to agreeing upon:
   a. Details of the transitional regime.
   b. Timetable for the Israeli withdrawal.
   c. Mutual security arrangements for all the parties concerned during and following the transitional period.
   d. Modalities for the implementation of relevant UN resolutions on Palestinian refugees.
   e. Other issues considered appropriate by all parties.

4. Israel shall withdraw from the West Bank (including/East/Jerusalem) and the Gaza Strip, occupied since June 1967. The Israeli withdrawal applies to the settlements established in the occupied territories.

5. The Israeli military government in the West Bank and the Gaza Strip shall be abolished at the outset of the transitional period. Supervision over the administration of the West Bank shall become the responsibility of Jordan and supervision over the administration of the Gaza strip shall become the responsibility of Egypt. Jordan and Egypt shall carry out their responsibility in cooperation with freely elected representatives of the Palestinian people who shall exercise direct authority over the administration of the West Bank and Gaza. The UN shall supervise and facilitate the Israeli withdrawal and the restoration of Arab authority.

6. Egypt and Jordan shall guarantee that the security arrangements to be agreed upon will continue to be respected in the West Bank and Gaza.

Appendix III

Camp David Agreement: Framework for West Bank and Gaza, September, 1978

. . . The parties are determined to reach a just, comprehensive, and durable settlement of the Middle East conflict through the conclusion of peace treaties based on Security Council Resolutions 242 and 338 in all their parts. Their purpose is to achieve peace and good neighborly relations. They recognize that, for peace to endure, it must involve all those who have been most deeply affected by the conflict. They therefore agree that this framework as appropriate is intended by them to constitute a basis for peace not only between Egypt and Israel, but also between Israel and each of its other neighbors which is prepared to negotiate peace with Israel on this basis. With that objective in mind, they have agreed to proceed as follows:

A. West Bank and Gaza

1. Egypt, Israel, Jordan and the representatives of the Palestinian people should participate in negotiations on the resolution of the Palestinian problem in all its aspects. To achieve that objective, negotiations relating to the West Bank and Gaza should proceed in three stages:

(a) Egypt and Israel agree that, in order to ensure a peaceful and orderly transfer of authority, and taking into account the security concerns of all the parties, there should be transitional arrangements for the West Bank and Gaza for a period not exceeding five years. In order to provide full autonomy to the inhabitants, under these arrangements the Israeli military government and its civilian administration will be withdrawn as soon as a self-governing authority has been freely elected by the inhabitants of these areas to replace the existing military government. To negotiate the details of a transitional arrangement, the Government of Jordan will be invited to join the negotiations on the basis of this framework. These new arrangements should give due consideration both to the principle of self-government by the inhabitants of these territories and to the legitimate security concerns of the parties involved.

(b) Egypt, Israel, and Jordan will agree on the modalities for establishing the elected self-governing authority in the West Bank and Gaza. The delegations of Egypt and Jordan may include Palestinians from the West Bank and Gaza or other Palestinians as mutually agreed. The parties

will negotiate an agreement which will define the powers and responsibilities of the self-governing authority to be exercised in the West Bank
and Gaza. A withdrawal of Israeli armed forces will take place and
there will be a redeployment of the remaining Israeli forces into specified
security locations. The agreement will also include arrangements for
assuring internal and external security and public order. A strong local
police force will be established, which may include Jordanian citizens.
In addition, Israeli and Jordanian forces will participate in joint patrols
and in the manning of control posts to assure the security of the borders.

(c) When the self-governing authority (administrative council) in the
West Bank and Gaza is established and inaugurated, the transitional
period of five years will begin. As soon as possible, but not later than
the third year after the beginning of the transitional period, negotiations
will take place to determine the final status of the West Bank and Gaza
and its relationship with its neighbors, and to conclude a peace treaty
between Israel and Jordan by the end of the transitional period. These
negotiations will be conducted among Egypt, Israel, Jordan, and the
elected representatives of the inhabitants of the West Bank and Gaza.
Two separate but related committees will be convened, one committee,
consisting of representatives of the four parties which will negotiate
and agree on the final status of the West Bank and Gaza, and its
relationship with its neighbors, and the second committee, consisting
of representatives of Israel and representatives of Jordan to be joined
by the elected representatives of the inhabitants of the West Bank and
Gaza, to negotiate the peace treaty between Israel and Jordan, taking
into account the agreement reached on the final status of the West Bank
and Gaza. The negotiations shall be based on all the provisions and
principles of UN Security Council Resolution 242. The negotiations
will resolve, among other matters, the location of the boundaries and
the nature of the security arrangements. The solution from the negotiations must also recognize the legitimate rights of the Palestinian
people and their just requirements. In this way, the Palestinians will
participate in the determination of their own future through:

1) The negotiations among Egypt, Israel, Jordan and the representatives of the inhabitants of the West Bank and Gaza to agree on the
final status of the West Bank and Gaza and other outstanding issues
by the end of the transitional period.

2) Submitting their agreement to a vote by the elected representatives
of the inhabitants of the West Bank and Gaza.

3) Providing for the elected representatives of the inhabitants of the
West Bank and Gaza to decide how they shall govern themselves consistent
with the provisions of their agreement.

4) Participating as stated above in the work of the committee negotiating the peace treaty between Israel and Jordan.

2. All necessary measures will be taken and provisions made to assure the security of Israel and its neighbors during the transitional period and beyond. To assist in providing such security, a strong local police force will be constituted by the self-governing authority. It will be composed of inhabitants of the West Bank and Gaza. The police will maintain continuing liaison on internal security matters with the designated Israeli, Jordanian, and Egyptian officers.

3. During the transitional period, representatives of Egypt, Israel, Jordan, and the self-governing authority will constitute a continuing committee to decide by agreement on the modalities of admission of persons displaced from the West Bank and Gaza in 1967, together with necessary measures to prevent disruption and disorder. Other matters of common concern may also be dealt with by this committee.

4. Egypt and Israel will work with each other and with other interested parties to establish agreed procedures for a prompt, just and permanent implementation of the resolution of the refugee problem.

Source: U.S. Department of State, *The Camp David Summit September 1978,* Dept. of State pub. 8954, N.E. & South Asian Series 88.

Appendix IV

Agreement Between King Hussein of Jordan and Yasir Arafat, Chairman of the P.L.O., February 11, 1985

Emanating from the spirit of the Fez summit resolutions, approved by Arab states, and from United Nations resolutions relating to the Palestine question,

In accordance with international legitimacy, and

Deriving from a common understanding on the establishment of a special relationship between the Jordanian and Palestinian peoples,

The Government of the Hashemite Kingdom of Jordan and the Palestine Liberation Organization have agreed to move together toward the achievement of a peaceful and just settlement of the Middle East crisis and the termination of Israeli occupation of the occupied Arab territories, including Jerusalem, on the basis of the following principles:

1. Total withdrawal from the territories occupied in 1967 for comprehensive peace as established in United Nations and Security Council resolutions.

2. Right of self-determination for the Palestinian people: Palestinians will exercise their inalienable right of self-determination when Jordanians

and Palestinians will be able to do so within the context of the formation of the proposed confederated Arab states of Jordan and Palestine.

3. Resolution of the problem of Palestinian refugees in accordance with United Nations resolutions.

4. Resolution of the Palestine question in all its aspects.

5. And on this basis, peace negotiatins will be conducted under the auspices of an international conference in which the five permanent members of the Security Council and all the parties to the conflict will participate, including the Palestine Liberation Organization, the sole legitimate representative of the Palestine people, within a joint delegation (joint Jordanian-Palestinian delegation).

Source: Translation by Jordan's Acting Information Minister, Taher Hikmat, in *The New York Times,* Feb. 12, 1985, p. 12.

Appendix V

President Ronald Reagan Proposals for Middle East Peace,
September 1, 1982

What are the specific new American positions, and why are we taking them?

In the Camp David talks thus far, both Israel and Egypt have felt free to express openly their views as to what the outcome should be. Understandably, their views have differed on many points.

The United States has thus far sought to play the role of mediator: we have avoided public comment on the key issues. We have always recognized—and continue to recognize—that only the voluntary agreement of those parties most directly involved in the conflict can provide an enduring solution. But it has become evident to me that some clearer sense of America's position on the key issues is necessary to encourage wider support for the peace process.

First, as outlined in the Camp David accords, there must be a period of time during which the Palestinian inhabitants of the West Bank and Gaza will have full autonomy over their own affairs. Due consideration must be given to the principle of self-government by the inhabitants of the territories and to the legitimate security concerns of the parties involved.

The purpose of the 5-year period of transition, which would begin after free elections for a self-governing Palestinian authority, is to prove to the Palestinians that they can run their own affairs and that such Palestinian autonomy poses no threat to Israel's security.

The United States will not support the use of any additional land for the purpose of settlements during the transition period. Indeed, the immediate adoption of a settlement freeze by Israel, more than any other action, could create the confidence needed for wider participation in these talks. Further settlement activity is in no way necessary for the security of Israel and only diminishes the confidence of the Arabs that a final outcome can be freely and fairly negotiated.

I want to make the American position well understood: The purpose of this transition period is the peaceful and orderly transfer of authority from Israel to the Palestinian inhabitants of the West Bank and Gaza. At the same time, such a transfer must not interfere with Israel's security requirements.

Beyond the transition period, as we look to the future of the West Bank and Gaza, it is clear to me that peace cannot be achieved by the formation of an independent Palestinian state in those territories. Nor is it achievable on the basis of Israeli sovereignty or permanent control over the West Bank and Gaza.

So the United States will not support the establishment of an independent Palestinian state in the West Bank and Gaza, and we will not support annexation or permanent control by Israel.

There is, however, another way to peace. The final status of these lands must, of course, be reached through the give-and-take of negotiations. But it is the firm view of the United States that self-government by the Palestinians of the West Bank and Gaza in association with Jordan offers the best chance for a durable, just and lasting peace.

We base our approach squarely on the principle that the Arab-Israeli conflict should be resolved through negotiations involving an exchange of territory for peace. This exchange is enshrined in U.N. Security Council Resolution 242, which is, in turn, incorporated in all its parts in the Camp David agreements. U.N. Resolution 242 remains wholly valid as the foundation stone of America's Middle East peace effort.

It is the United States' position that—in return for peace—the withdrawal provision of Resolution 242 applies to all fronts, including the West Bank and Gaza.

When the border is negotiated between Jordan and Israel, our view on the extent to which Israel should be asked to give up territory will be heavily affected by the extent of true peace and normalization and the security arrangements offered in return.

Finally, we remain convinced that Jerusalem must remain undivided, but its final status should be decided through negotiations.

In the course of the negotiations to come, the United States will support positions that seem to us fair and reasonable compromises and likely to promote a sound agreement. We will also put forward our own detailed proposals when we believe they can be helpful. And, make no mistake, the United States will oppose any proposal—from any party and at any point in the negotiating process-that threatens the security of Israel. America's commitment to the security of Israel is ironclad. And, I might add, so is mine.

Source: U.S. Department of State, Bureau of Public Affairs, *Current Policy no. 417.*

Appendix VI

Principles on Arab-Israeli Conflict from Arab Summit Conference at Fez, September 6–9, 1982

1. The withdrawal of Israeli forces from all territories occupied in 1967, including Arab Jerusalem.
2. The dismantlement of the settlements established by Israel after 1967 in the Arab territories.
3. The guarantee of freedom of worship and the practice of religious rites for all religions in the Holy Places.
4. The re-affirmation of the right of the Palestinian people to self-determination and of the exercise of their imprescriptible and inalienable national rights under the leadership of the Palestine Liberation Organization, their legitimate and sole representative, and compensation for those who do not wish to return.
5. The West Bank and Gaza are to be placed under United Nations supervision for a transitional period not exceeding a few months.
6. The establishment of the independent Palestinian state with Jerusalem as its capital.
7. The United Nations Security Council is to establish peace guarantees for all states in the area, including the independent Palestinian state.
8. The United Nations Security Council is to guarantee the implementation of these principles.

Source: Translation from the Arabic version printed in *Al-Sharq Al-Awsat* (11.9.82), International Institute of Strategic Studies, *Survival,* Nov/Dec 1982, Vol. XXIV, No. 6.

Appendix VII

Text of United Nations Security Council Resolution 242, November 22, 1967

Adopted unanimously at the 1382nd meeting:

The Security Council,

Expressing its continuing concern with the grave situation in the Middle East, Emphasizing the inadmissibility of the acquisition of territory by war and the need to work for a just and lasting peace in which every State in the area can live in security,

Emphasizing further that all Member States in their acceptance of the Charter of the United Nations have undertaken a commitment to act in accordance with article 2 of Charter,

1. Affirms that the fulfillment of Charter principles requires the establishment of a just and lasting peace in the Middle East which should include the application of both the following principles:

(i) Withdrawal of Israeli armed forces from territories occupied in the recent conflict;

(ii) Termination of all claims or states of belligerency and respect for and acknowledgement of the sovereignty, territorial integrity and political independence of every State in the area and their right to live in peace within secure and recognized boundaries free from threats or acts of force;

2. Affirms further the necessity

(a) For guaranteeing freedom of navigation through international waterways in the area;

(b) For achieving a just settlement of the refugee problem;

(c) For guaranteeing the territorial inviolability and political independence of every State in the area, through measures including the establishment of demilitarized zones;

3. Requests the Secretary-General to designate a Special Representative to proceed to the Middle East to establish and maintain contacts with the States concerned in order to promote agreement and assist efforts to achieve a peaceful and accepted settlement in accordance with the provisions and principles of this resolution.

4. Requests the Secretary-General to report to the Security Council on the progress of the efforts of the Special Representative as soon as possible.

Text of United Nations Security Council Resolution 338,
October 21–22, 1973

Adopted at the 1747th meeting:

The Security Council,

1. Calls upon all parties to the present fighting to cease all firing and terminate all military activity immediately, no later than 12 hours after the moment of the adoption of this decision, in the positions they now occupy;

2. Calls upon the parties concerned to start immediately after the cease-fire the implementation of Security Council Resolution 242 (1967) in all of its parts;

3. Decides that, immediately and concurrently with the cease-fire, negotiations start between the parties concerned under appropriate auspices aimed at establishing a just and durable peace in the Middle East.

Source: U.S. Dept of State, Pub. 8954, Op. Cit.

Appendix VIII

Occupied Territories-Withdrawal or Occupation:
The Economic Consequences

Dr. Simcha Bahiri, who is engaged in economic-based peace research at Tel Aviv University, summarizes the findings of his extensive study, *Peaceful Separation or Enforced Unity: Economic Consequences for Israel and the West Bank/Gaza Area.* He concludes that Israel's political, demographic and economic structure would be significantly improved without the Territories.

If the West Bank and Gaza Strip were to be peacefully separated from Israel within the framework of an overall regional peace settlement, after a decade of peace Israel's gross civilian product (i.e. GNP less defense costs) could be 45% (or $10 billion) higher than that which may be expected if present trends continue. This and other projections were arrived at in the framework of a more extensive study by the author *(Peaceful Separation or Enforced Unity: Economic Consequences for Israel and the West Bank/Gaza Area,* International Center for Peace in the Middle East, Tel Aviv, 1984).

The two major projections involved the formulation of two alternative scenarios, or options: an "Israeli option" consisting of Israeli-dominated, enforced "unity" between Israel and West Bank/Gaza—i.e. a continuation of the present situation, with possible minor variations; and an option of separate development in which the West Bank and Gaza, either independently or in a loose union with Jordan, would be effectively severed from Israel. This second option does not rule out a degree of mutually beneficial and agreed upon economic cooperation.

The study, which is based on "exploratory forecasting" and which uses economic projection models, sets out the probable lines of development for each scenario. The following table summarizes and compares some of the more important ten-year projections for each scenario. 1985 is used as a base year for these economic forecasts which, at least for

Israel, are very conservative (that is, without peace the Israeli scenario could be worse in 1995, and with peace it could be better).

Given that domestic and international realities may make separation inevitable, the sooner such separation is implemented, the less costly it would be, the positive economic impact would be greater, and the development of a just economic interdependence leading to a strengthening of the vested interest in peace would be more likely.

The Options

The essence of the Israeli option or scenario is the continued and increased economic integration of the territories and Israel, combined with continued large-scale Jewish settlement. In the event of this development, the Arab population of "Greater Israel" (as compared with the present State of Israel) would triple by 1995 and would account for nearly 40% of the total population: there would be some four million Jews out of a total population of 6.62 million, including about 120,000 Jewish settlers in the occupied territories (excluding Jerusalem). Under this option, economic transactions with Jordan and the rest of the Arab world would be minimal. Israel's relations with its major aid and trading partners might be adversely affected, while net Jewish immigration would not exceed 5,000 per year and defense expenditure would increase at a slightly higher rate than that of the economy as a whole.

Under the separate option or scenario, economic relations between Israel and West Bank/Gaza at the end of the ten year transition period would be those of friendly neighboring states. Israel would achieve a higher rate of economic growth, investment and trade, while West Bank/Gaza would enjoy a considerable degree of economic integration with Jordan. Economic assistance would be provided by the Arab countries and by the West, while water resources would be made available for the expanded agricultural needs of West Bank/Gaza either from Lebanon (the Litani), Jordan (the Yarmuk) or Egypt (the Nile). A major assumption is that over 600,000 Palestinians would return and that the rest of the Palestinians would remain stateless. Palestinians would acquire the citizenship of the new entity; it should be noted that recent political moves by Jordan and the PLO, supported by other Arab states, indicate a willingness for a settlement of this nature.

The Israeli Economy: Alternative 1995 Scenarios

While the study also discusses economic alternatives for West Bank/Gaza (see table: note that the economic benefits and positive changes are greater for the West Bank in the event of a peaceful option—despite massive absorption difficulties—than they are for Israel), we will now concentrate on the effect of the alternative scenarios on the Israeli economy.

In general, it was found that despite the "benefits" gained from the exploitative nature of economic relations with the territories, Israel's political, demographic and economic structure would be more favorable without the territories.

In the event of the separate option—leading to regional peace—the Jewish population in 1995 might total 4.3 million, or 300,000 more than would be the case under continued Israeli rule over the territories and an absence of peace. The difference is accounted for by increased immigration (especially from the Soviet Union), decreased emigration, and by greater natural increase.

Israel's Arab population would be 100,000 less under the separate option, due mainly to possible border modifications around East Jerusalem. All told, by 1995 there would be an additional 300,000 Jews and 1.7 million fewer Arabs in the State of Israel than in "Greater Israel."

Today, West Bank/Gaza serves to some extent as a "labor barracks" for certain categories of less skilled work in Israel. While at present about 90,000 West Bank/Gaza residents cross over to work inside Israel, by 1995 their numbers would exceed 120,000. Under the separate option the increase in the native Israeli work force that would be necessitated by the gradual reduction of the number of workers from the territories (although 50,000 workers might still continue to work in Israel) could be achieved, *inter alia,* by (1) the gainful employment of a larger proportion of the population as a result of greater economic incentive; (2) less time spent in military service and reserve duty; and (3) increased immigration of high-level manpower. The gross domestic product per employed person (a measure of productivity) would be about one-sixth higher under the separate option.

In general, the separate option implies at least an equal and probably a higher level of security than does the Israeli option, and at defense costs reduced by 38% in absolute terms. (It is assumed that West Bank/Gaza would be effectively demilitarized. The absolute level of defense expenditure is not expected to decrease significantly). In terms of the percent of the GNP, defense costs would be 13% under the peaceful scenario and 26% under the Israeli option, the proportion in recent years. This does not take into account the greater likelihood of war if the territories are retained. A comprehensive peace settlement involving the two superpowers would lead to the normalization of relations not only with Israel's Arab neighbors, but also with the Soviet and Third World Blocs, and would entail guarantees from both superpowers. Eventually, under the separate option, there would be a smaller army, less reserve duty and higher morale. (The low morale of the troops in Lebanon and to a lesser extent in the West Bank should be noted. The latter would certainly increase with increased resistance in the territories).

The pre-condition for a regional peace settlement is the political separation of Israel and the occupied territories, i.e. "land for peace." This, in turn, would lead to a degree of economic cooperation, especially increased trade. The $100 billion market constituted by the region's Arab states could provide a potential for a radical increase in Israeli exports. All told, Israeli exports might well be 30% ($5 billion) higher under the separate option than they would be under the Israeli option, and there would be a $2.5 billion reduction in the trade deficit as well.

Given a peaceful resolution of the Palestinian problem resulting in the establishment of a Palestinian entity separate from Israel, Israel's per annum GNP growth rate would reach at least 5.7%, versus a maximum of 3.5% if the present trend continues. The increase in the per capita GNP would be 3.6% per annum under the separate option, nearly double that under the Israeli option (1.9%). The gross civilian product, as stated earlier, would be 45% higher under the separate option. It is striking that the GNP forecast for Israel alone (separate option) is actually $5 billion higher than that forecast for Israel plus West Bank/Gaza ("Greater Israel"), a tendency that is manifested by all other major economic indicators as well. A close examination of the table will indicate the massive economic benefits (and these are conservative projections) of a peaceful settlement of the Israel-Palestine problem to both potential peace partners.

Political Comparisons and Economic Potential

In 1962, when Algeria finally won independence from France, over one million French settlers, some of whom had roots going back several generations, returned to France. They represented one-eight of the population of Algeria (the Jewish population of West Bank/Gaza is only 3%), and 2% of the population of "metropolitan" France (the settler equivalent for "Greater Israel" is only just over 1%).

A similar situation occurred a decade later when hundreds of thousands of Portuguese settlers left the ex-colonies of Angola and Mozambique, despite their formal official status as parts of "metropolitan" Portugal.

A high degree of mutually beneficial economic cooperation was established between the former colonial powers of France and Portugal and the newly independent former colonies. This occurred after and despite protracted wars and often fierce resistance from the former settlers. If domestic and international realities are considered, together with the economic, political, demographic and social consequences of retaining the territories, it will be seen that the sooner separation is implemented, the less costly it will be. The economic benefits accruing to both parties in the dispute would far exceed the cost of vacating the area—even in view of the (unnecessary) precedent established by the exorbitant reparations paid to the settlers who evacuated the Yamit area, and the loss to Israel of some over-exploitative economic benefits which resulted from the colonial-type relationship with the territories.

The economic benefits and interdependence generated by real cooperation would give each of the parties a vested interest in peace and would raise the future cost of dissociation. Israel, West Bank/Gaza, and possibly Jordan could together serve as a technological transfer center and economic entrepot for the entire hinterland (including the oil-rich states). In contrast, "Greater Israel" would be isolated from its potential regional partners (and from other areas) and would continue to live in an area of hostility rather than in a more prosperous sea of tranquility. Choice is still possible.

Source: Simha Bahiri, "Occupied Territories Withdrawal or Occupation The Economic Consequences," *New Outlook,* May/June 1985.

TABLE A-1
1985-95 Forecasts for Israel and West Bank/Gaza (US$ 1982)

	1985 Israel	1985 WBG	1985 Israel Option Israel	1985 Israel Option WBG
A. Population & Employment(thousands)				
1. Average population	4,270	1,300	5,000	1,620
2. Average Jewish population	3,500	(40)	4,000	(120)
3. Employment	1,370	240*	1,700	300
B. Distribution of GNP & Resources ($ million)				
4. Gross National Product (GNP)	23,000	1,640	32,500	2,500
5. Defense Expenditure (D)	5,800	--	8,450	--
6. Governmental Civilian Consumption(Gc)	2,500	150	3,570	225
7. Private Consumption	14,500	1,230	19,180	1,850
8. Investment (I)	5,500	340	7,800	525
9. Resources (R=D+Gc+P+I)	28,300	1,720	39,000	2,600
10. Trade Surplus (TS=GNP-R)	-5,300	+80	-6,500	-100
11. Exports of Goods & Services (exc. labor)	10,000	480	16,000	700
12. Gross Domestic Savings(I+IS)	+200	+260	+1,300	+425
13. Gross Civilian Product (GCP=GNP-D)	17,200	1,640	24,050	2,500
C. Per Capita Indices ($)				
14. GNP/Capita	5,390	1,280	6,500	1,540
15. GNP/employment	16,970	6,830	19,230	8,330
16. Defense/capita	1,360	--	1,690	--
17. Private Consumption/capita	3,400	950	3,840	1,140
D. Ten Year Growth Indices (% per annum)				
18. Population	2.1	2.1	1.6	2.2
19. Jewish population	1.8	(20.0)	1.3	(12.0)
20. Employment	2.0	1.6	2.2	2.2
21. GNP	2.3	3.4	3.5	4.5
22. Defense Expenditure	-1.5**	--	3.8	--
23. Government Civilian Consumption	6.0	1.8	3.6	4.1
24. Private consumption	4.0	3.2	2.8	4.2
25. Investment	-0.9	1.5	3.6	4.4
26. Exports	5.5	3.9	4.8	3.8

*Includes 90,500 working in Israel.
**The 1975 level of defense expenditure was at an especially high level following the 1973 Yom Kippur War.

TABLE A-1 (continued)

	1995 Separate Option		1995 Difference (SO/IO in %)	
	Israel	WBG	Israel	WBG (% difference)
A. Population & Employment(thousands)				
1. Average population	5,200	2,560	4.0	58.0
2. Average Jewish population	4,300	--	7.5	--
3. Employment	1,800	450	6.5	50.0
B. Distribution of GNP & Resources ($ million)				
4. Gross National Product (GNP)	40,000	4,300	23.1	72.0
5. Defense Expenditure (D)	5,200	100	-38.5	--
6. Governmental Civilain Consumption(Gc)	4,400	730	-23.2	224.4
7. Private Consumption	23,200	3,010	21.0	62.7
8. Investment (I)	11,200	1,560	43.6	197.1
9. Resources (R=D+Gc+P+I)	44,000	5,300	12.8	103.8
10. Trade Surplus (TS=GNP-R)	-4,000	-1,000	+38.5	-900.0
11. Exports of Goods & Service (exc. labor)	21,000	1,300	31.3	85.7
12. Gross Domestic Savings (I+IS)	+7,200	+560	+453.8	31.8
13. Gross Civilian Product (GCP=GNP-D)	34,800	4,200	44.7	68.0
C. Per Capita Indices ($)				
14. GNP/Capita	7,690	1,680		
15. GNP/employmnet	22,220	9,560	15.5	14.8
16. Defense/capita	1,000	39	-40.8	--
17. Private Consumption/capita	4,460	1,175	+16.1	3.1

			1995 Difference in %	
18. Population	2.0	7.0	0.4	4.8
19. Jewish population	2.1	--	0.9	--
20. Employment	2.9	6.5	0.7	4.3
21. GNP	5.7	10.1	2.2	5.6
22. Defense Expenditure	0.2	--	4.0	--
23. Government Civilian Consumption	5.8	17.1	2.2	13.0
24. Private consumption	4.8	9.4	2.0	5.2
25. Investment	7.4	16.4	3.8	12.0
26. Exports	7.7	10.5	2.9	6.7

Source: Simha Bahiri, "Occupied Territories Withdrawal or Occupation The Economic Consequences," New Outlook, May/June 1985

Selected Bibliography

Books, Monographs, and Studies

Abu-Lughod, Ibrahim, ed. *The Transformation of Palestine.* Evanston, Ill.: Northwestern University Press, 1971.

Aruri, Naseer H. *Jordan: A Study in Political Development (1921-1965).* The Hague: Martinus Nijhoff, 1972.

Awartani, Hisham. *A Survey of Industries in the West Bank and Gaza Strip.* Birzeit: Birzeit University, 1979.

Benvenisti, Meron. *The West Bank Data Project A Survey Of Israel's Policies.* Washington, D.C.: American Enterprise Institute, 1984.

Bregman, Arie, *Economic Growth of the Administered Areas, 1968-1973.* Jerusalem: Bank of Israel, 1975.

———. *The Economy of the Administered Territories, 1974-1975.* Jerusalem: Bank of Israel, 1976.

Bull, Vivian. *The West Bank: Is It Viable?* Lexington, Mass.: Lexington Books, 1975.

Cohen, Amnon. *Political Parties in the West Bank Under the Jordanian Regime, 1949-1967.* Ithaca: Cornell University Press, 1982.

Elazar, Daniel J., ed. *Self Rule/Shared Rule: Federal solutions to the Middle East Conflict.* Ramat Gan: Turtledove, 1979.

———. *Judea, Samaria, and Gaza: Views on the Present and future.* Washington, D.C.: American Enterprise Institute, 1982.

ESCO Foundation for Palestine. *Palestine A Study of Jewish, Arab, and British Policies.* 2 vols. New Haven: Yale University Press, 1947.

Gharaibeh, Fawzi A. *The Economies of the West Bank and Gaza Strip.* Boulder: Westview Press, 1985.

Granott, A. *The Land System in Palestine History and Structure.* London: Eyre and Spottiswoode, 1952.

Gubser, Peter. *Jordan, Crossroads of Middle Eastern Events.* Boulder: Westview Press, 1983.

Halabi, Rafik. *The West Bank Story.* New York: Harcourt Brace Jovanovich, 1981.

Harris, William Wilson. *Taking Root Israeli Settlement in the West Bank, the Golan and Gaza-Sinai, 1967-1980.* New York: John Wiley (Research Studies Press), 1980.

Heller, Mark A. *A Palestinian State The Implications for Israel.* Cambridge, Mass: Harvard University Press, 1983.

Hurewitz, J.C. *The Struggle for Palestine.* New York: W. W. Norton, 1950.

Isaac, Rael Jean. *Israel Divided: Ideological Politics in the Jewish State.* Baltimore: The Johns Hopkins University Press, 1978.

Ishaq, J. and Smith, C. *Demography of the Palestinians Part One The West Bank.* Bethlehem: Bethlehem University, 1982.

Israel Government. *Census of Population 1967 West Bank of the Jordan Gaza Strip and Northern Sinai Golan Heights.* Jerusalem: Central Bureau of Statistics (CBS), 1967.

――――. *Housing Conditions, Household Equipment, Welfare Assistance & Farming in the Administered Areas.* Jerusalem: CBS, 1967.

――――. *Demographic Characteristics of the Population in the Administered Areas.* Jerusalem: CBS, 1967.

――――. *Labour Force Part I.* Jerusalem: CBS, 1967.

――――. *Census of Population and Housing 1967 East Jerusalem.* Jerusalem: CBS, 1968.

――――. *Statistical Abstract of Israel 1967.* Jerusalem: CBS, 1967―.

――――. *Judea-Samaria and the Gaza District A sixteen-Year Survey (1967-1983).* Jerusalem: Ministry of Defense, November 1983.

Kanovsky, Eliahu. *The Economic Impact of the Six Day War.* New York: Praeger, 1970.

Kimmerling, Baruch. *Zionism and Territory The Socio-Territorial Dimensions of Zionist Politics.* Berkeley: Univ. of California (Institute of International Studies), 1983.

Lesch, Ann Mosely. *Arab Politics in Palestine 1917-1939 The Frustration of a Nationalist Movement.* Ithaca: Cornell University Press, 1979.

――――. *Political Perceptions of the Palestinians on the West Bank and the Gaza Strip.* Washington, D. C.: The Middle East Institute, 1980.

Mazur, Michael P. *Economic Growth and Development of Jordan.* Boulder: Westview Press, 1979.

Migdal, Joel S., et al. *Palestinian Society and Politics.* Princeton: Princeton University Press, 1980.

Mishal, Shaul. *West Bank/East Bank: The Palestinians in Jordan 1949-1967.* New Haven: Yale University Press, 1978.

Nakleh, Emile A., ed. *A Palestinian Agenda for the West Bank and Gaza.* Washington, D.C.: American Enterprise Institute, 1980.

Nathan, Robert R.; Gass, Oscar; Creamer, Daniel. *Palestine: Problem and Promise an Economic Study.* Washington, D.C.: Public Affairs Press, 1946.

Nisan, Mordechai. *Israel and the Territories: A Study in Control 1967-1977.* Ramat Gan: Turtledove, 1978.

Peretz, Don. *A Palestine Entity?* Washington, D.C.: The Middle East Institute, 1970.

Plascov, Avi. *The Palestinian Refugees in Jordan 1948-57.* London: Frank Cass, 1981.

Polk, William R.; Stamler, David; Asfour, Edmund. *Backdrop to Tragedy The Struggle for Palestine.* Boston: Beacon, 1957.

Porat, Yehoshua. *The Emergence of the Palestinian Arab National Movement, 1918-1929.* London: Frank Cass, 1974.

———. *The Palestinian Arab National Movement 1929-1939.* London: Frank Cass, 1978.

Quandt, William B.; Jabber, Fuad; and Lesch, Ann Mosely. *The Politics of Palestinian Nationalism.* Berkeley: University of California Press, 1973.

Richardson, John P. *The West Bank: A Portrait.* Washington, D.C.: The Middle East Institute, 1984.

Sandler, Shmuel, and Frisch, Hillel. *Israel, The Palestinians and the West Bank.* Lexington, Mass: Lexington Books, 1984.

Schnall, David J. *Radical Dissent in Contemporary Israeli Politics: Cracks in the Wall.* New York: Praeger, 1979.

Shalev, Arieh. *The Autonomy—Problems and Possible Solutions.* Tel Aviv: Center for Strategic Studies, Tel Aviv University, January 1980.

Shwadran, Benjamin. *Jordan A State of Tension* New York: Council for Middle Eastern Affairs Press, 1959.

Sinai, Anne, and Pollack, Allen, eds. *The Hashemite Kingdom of Jordan and the West Bank.* New York: American Academic Association for Peace in the Middle East, 1977.

Thorpe, Merle, Jr. *Prescription for Conflict Israel's West Bank Settlement Policy.* Washington, D.C.: Foundation for Middle East Peace, 1984.

Van Arkadie, Brian. *Benefits and Burdens: A Report on the West Bank and Gaza Strip Economics Since 1967.* New York: Carnegie Endowment for International Peace, 1977.

Vatikiotis, P.J. *Politics and the Military in Jordan, a Study of the Arab Legion 1921-1957.* London; Frank Cass, 1967.

Ward, Richard J.; Peretz, Don; Wilson, Evan M. *The Palestine State A Rational Approach.* Port Washington, N.Y.: Kennikat Press, 1977.

Periodicals

Israel Economist
Jerusalem Quarterly
Jerusalem Post International Edition
Journal of Palestine Studies
MERIP Reports
Middle East Journal
New Outlook

Index

ε